triathlon

SERIOUS ABOUT YOUR SPORT

Adam Dickson, Remmert Wielinga, Paul Cowcher and Tommaso Bernabei

Additional writing by Russell Murphy, Nic Newell, Dan Cross, Daniel Ford and Adam Hathaway

Contents

Introduction

Following two massive brain seizures in April 2004, the Orthopaedic Consultant at Royal Bournemouth Hospital in England informed me I needed an operation to remove dead muscle in my legs, caused by the trauma. The significance of this didn't register at first, as I had already spent several weeks in hospital. Only after the operation did reality sink in and I realized the full extent of my injuries.

The seizures had cut off the circulation to my lower legs, causing a condition called Compartment Syndrome. The tendons in both ankles had been severed, leaving me with Drop Foot, an inability to raise my feet using the normal ankle reflex. From then on I had to rely on crutches and uncomfortable plastic ankle supports to get from A to B.

As a lifelong runner and fitness enthusiast, I was now facing the future as a cripple. Determined not to let my disability affect my overall quality of life, I began a gentle exercise regime of cycling and swimming. My dad had been a member of the British Army Water Polo Team and had taught me to swim early on, so at least I had this to fall back on.

The crutches and ankle supports soon went and I found that with a little effort I could walk unaided. One morning, out walking along one of my old running tracks, I decided to test my progress and broke into a light jog. That moment was the turning point in my rehabilitation and proved that, in spite of my injuries, I could still run, even if it was only to the end of the road.

My fitness improved and soon I was running, cycling and swimming on a regular basis. The owner of a local running shop suggested I take part in a triathlon and, with some trepidation, I agreed. I loved the sport from the start and entered as many events as I could, gaining experience and learning to overcome the fears I had around my disability.

After running the London Marathon in 2006, I set my sights a little higher and entered what many regard as the toughest one-day sporting event in the world. In August the following year, after 14 hours and 50 minutes, I crossed the finish line at Ironman UK.

Triathlon: Serious About Your Sport is aimed at anyone who wants to improve their knowledge of triathlon and explore their potential. Whether you are a swimmer, cyclist or runner looking to branch out from your specialist sport or a triathlete looking for improvement, this book will guide you through the process.

The basics section, which sets out what lies ahead in terms of training and conditioning for this sport, is followed by a comprehensive look at Technique & tactics, which focuses on the individual skills needed for each discipline and how to combine them in training and in races.

Sections on Fitness & training and Cross training look at ways of fine-tuning your body using sport specific workouts and strengthening exercises that are geared to the demands of triathlon.

Nutrition and fuelling are crucial to success, particularly in long-distance triathlons. Getting to know your body's needs in training will help you maintain a good, healthy diet and improve your energy levels.

The Training programmes cover four triathlon distances: Sprint, Olympic, Half-Ironman and Ironman for four levels of ability ranging from unfit beginner to advanced.

Triathlon is a wonderful, life-affirming sport that will both challenge and enhance your current exercise regime. It is my sincere wish that you use the contents of this book to enjoy many seasons of swimming, cycling and running.

Adam Dickson (July 2011)

the basics

// GETTING STARTED
// TRAINING PRINCIPLES
// SLEEP, FOOD, FLUID

Getting started

Triathlon combines swimming, cycling and running in a single event. As the timer runs from start to finish, with no breaks in-between, all your training will need to be geared specifically for this. Most newcomers find the transition from one discipline to the next the hardest aspect to cope with, so the more you practise in training, the better prepared you will be on the day of the race. Writing out a checklist of what you need to do at each transition will help you familiarize yourself with the process and the various items you will need at each transition.

Take time to learn the basic techniques associated with each discipline. Lessons from a qualified swimming instructor will help improve things like stroke, breathing and streamlining, although these will need to be adapted if your race starts in open water. Combined cycling and running workouts will prepare your leg muscles for transition, so practise a smooth pedal stroke on your bike, while a sound, economical running style will keep fatigue at bay and increase your performance overall.

The key element in any triathlon is endurance. Race distances vary depending on the event (see chart on Triathlon distances), meaning you could be racing from anything from two to 17 hours. Structure your training accordingly and use one session per week in each discipline to build endurance specifically for the length of the race you've en-

Triathlon distances
Sprint

750 metres (0.46 miles)*	Swim
20 km (12.42 miles)	Cycle
5 km (3.1 miles)	Run

Olympic

1.5 km (0.93 miles)	Swim
40 km (24.8 miles)	Cycle
10 km (6.2 miles)	Run

Half-Ironman

1.9 km (1.2 miles)	Swim
90 km (56 miles)	Cycle
21.1 km (13.1 miles)	Run

Ironman

3.86 km (2.4 miles)	Swim
180.25 km (112 miles)	Cycle
42.2 km (26.2 miles)	Run

Note: these are the standard accepted race distances but you will find triathlons of varying distances. Ironman is a brand name owned by the World Triathlon Corporation. Although other triathlons are competed over this distance they are not Ironman races.
* For indoor water swims this distance is usually 400 metres (0.25 miles).

tered. These longer workouts should be performed at a moderate pace that doesn't overtax your aerobic system and leave you exhausted.

Success in triathlon means pacing yourself correctly throughout. Work on your fuelling needs early on, but to safeguard your digestive system, only experiment with new products in training and not on race day. Keep the twin factors of pacing and fuelling uppermost in your mind, as this could mean the difference between success and failure on the big day. Ask yourselves questions in training, such as, "Could I run on these legs?" especially during long bike rides where you may be pushing too big a gear and wasting vital energy.

And last of all, that word often quoted but much ignored – rest. You can have the best coaches, the best equipment and the best training environment in the world, but skip this part of the programme and you'll pay heavily. Learn to train smart and enjoy many long and healthy seasons, in and out of the saddle. Remember too that rest also means relaxation, so find ways to unwind, that don't include physical pursuits such as gardening or painting the house! Most of all enjoy the thrill of taking part in a tough but rewarding experience that you'll probably want to repeat again and again.

The principles of training

The **SPORT** principles of training are aimed at helping you understand the training process and allowing you to plan your training so you see a steady upward progression in results.

Specificity – making sure your training is specific to what you are hoping to achieve. Simply put, don't spend all your time doing sprint training sets if you want to improve your long-distance running!

Progression – the body adapts to increased training loads and this will result in improved fitness levels and competitive performance.

Overload – training at a level that will push you. If you are always training at the same intensity and at the same speed you will not see the progression you would hope for. You need to be constantly overloading your muscles and cardio respiratory system to improve your strength and fitness level.

Reversibility – if you don't train or you decrease your intensity then you will see your fitness levels drop and as a consequence so will your overall performance. If you are unwell and are unable to train for an extended period then you will notice a reduced performance level when you start training again.

Tedium – keeping the training interesting. If you find yourself getting bored then you are less likely to want to train and your motivation levels will automatically drop, which can lead to a reduced effort level and even the likelihood of skipping training sessions. This will lead to Reversibility occurring.

When you start to plan your training programme you can use the FITT principles to work towards SPORT. For instance, to make sure that the SPORT principles of Progression and Overload are always occurring you can increase the Frequency

of your training sessions, the Intensity of each session or the Time you spend training. To stop Reversibility occurring rapidly you reduce Intensity if feeling sick. To avoid the SPORT principle of Tedium you can change the Type of training methods you are using. It is advisable that you only change one aspect of the training at a time rather than changing everything otherwise it can be too much for your body and may lead to an injury occurring.

Frequency – how often you train.

Intensity – intensity you train at.

Time – how long you train for.

Type – which training methods you are using.

Sleep, food and fluid

Getting your work-to-rest ratio right is crucial, as an imbalance will lead to over-training, which may result in a decreased performance in training and racing, as well as an increased chance of injury. Put simply: rest is as important as the training itself. As you get fitter you will be able to train longer as long as you keep getting quality rest.

- Set a schedule: be strict in your sleep regime. Sleep and wake at the same time every day including weekends and try to get at least eight hours of rest. Disrupting this schedule may lead to insomnia. 'Catching up' by sleeping extra on weekends makes it harder to wake up early on Monday morning because it re-sets your sleep cycles.

- Exercise: daily exercise will help you sleep, although a workout too close to your bedtime may disrupt your sleep. For maximum benefit try to get your exercise about five to six hours before going to bed.

- Avoid caffeine, nicotine, and alcohol. Don't take these stimulants close to your bedtime. Remember there is caffeine in coffee, chocolate, soft drinks, non-herbal teas, diet drugs and some pain relievers. Don't smoke a cigarette before going to bed as nicotine goes straight to the sleep centres of your brain and will result in a bad night's rest. Alcohol can decrease the time required to fall asleep. However, too much alcohol consumed within an hour of bedtime will deprive you of deep sleep and REM sleep (the sleep that rejuvenates your body the best) and it will keep you in the lighter stages of sleep.

- Relax before bed: reading, listening to music, having sex, taking a warm bath, can all make it easier to fall asleep. You can train yourself to associate certain activities with sleep and make them part of your bedtime ritual. If you can't get to sleep, don't just lie in bed – relax and do something else (like the previously mentioned activities) until you feel tired.

- Control your room temperature: make sure that you sleep in a room that is cool – 18-19 °C (64-66 °F) with 65 per cent of humidity is ideal – as well as dark and quiet.

So train hard and rest well. Nutrition can help supplement your training by giving you the right balance of energy to train and the proteins, vitamins and minerals to help you recover. If you are not getting the right levels of carbohydrates, proteins, fats and vitamins you will quickly feel tired in training and will fail to recover properly, which can lead to fatigue and maybe illness and injury. Hydration is critical, as the body has to be topped up to perform at its peak. Even a one per cent drop in hydration levels will impair your performance. Get used to taking on fluids.

Equipment

Swimming

That'll be a costume and some water then. It can be as simple as that but using the right equipment can make your swimming training a lot more effective and enjoyable and it also allows for you to add variety to each training session. The basics are a suitable swimming costume (you'll need a decent wetsuit if you are swimming in open water), a pair of goggles, a swimming cap and a drinks bottle. Some people don't like swimming caps but they do aid streamlining and for safety reasons increase your visibility in open water.

Other pieces of training equipment include a kick board and a pull buoy. These items allow you to isolate areas of each stroke and work them on their own. You can use a kick board to work on your leg kick to perfect technique. Remember that for triathletes the aim is an economical leg kick to conserve energy for what is ahead. A pull buoy is used to work on the arm-stroke technique. By isolating parts of your stroke you can make your training more challenging as you are trying to propel yourself through the water with only half the usual power.

If you want to make your training even more challenging you can wear hand paddles; these will allow you to put greater pressure on the water and therefore greater pressure on the arms and shoulders. Paddles should only be worn if you are already achieving good stroke technique and you need to take your training to the next level. You must also make sure that you build up gradually to avoid any shoulder injuries. When using paddles you should select the right paddles for your experience level as they come in different shapes and sizes, with the bigger paddles putting more pressure on the stroke.

A pair of fins can be used when concentrating on your kicking as well as being used for full-stroke swims. Wearing fins can make swimming full-stroke swims easier, which means you are able to focus on stroke technique. They also mean you are able to cover more distance and spend more time working on your technique.

Remember that tri suits, made of race-specific materials, can be worn throughout all three disciplines. This cuts down on time spent in the transitions as you will not need to change clothing. Check these out to see if they suit your needs.

Cycling

The correct position on the bike

If you want to get the most out of your cycling then finding your correct position on the bike is paramount. Cycling comfort and efficiency begin with a bike that fits. Getting your position correct means you are able to produce more power efficiently without working any muscles unnecessarily. Correct positioning of hands, feet and body are essential for success and avoiding injury. If you have back, neck, shoulder or knee pain, saddle sores or finger numbness, then your bike probably doesn't fit you.

We are all very different, each of us with different sizes of arms, legs, torsos and other parts of the body. All these factors must be evaluated when you seek to find your correct position on the bike. The following are some basic recommendations to provide you with a nearly perfect set-up. With experience you can then slightly adjust this position to meet your own requirements.

Frame size

To start in getting the right bike size, stand over the frame with your bare feet flat on the ground. A correctly sized road bike frame should give two and a half to five centimetres (one to two inches) of clearance between the top tube of the frame and your crotch. A more precise method to calculate the frame size is the formula: inseam length x 0.64.

The result of this formula is unequivocally correct but it's important to realize it pertains to traditional frame geometry. This is the conventional way of measuring the frame size 'centre to centre', which indicates the length of the seat tube from the centre of the bottom bracket to the centre of the seat lug (the point at which the centre line of the seat tube and the centre line of the top tube cross each other). Other ways to measure the size of a frame are:

Centre to top

Centre to top indicates the length of the seat tube from the centre of the bottom bracket to the top side of the seat lug. As a rule, this frame size should equal the centre-to-centre size, plus 15 to 20 millimetres (about three quarters of an inch).

Compact frame size

Many bike manufacturers specify the frame size of their sloping/compact frames according to the length of the seat tube, measured centre to centre as well as from centre to top. The frame size is then usually not specified as a numeric value but is simply expressed as 'small, medium, or large'. The problem with this way of measuring is that it turns out to be complicated to precisely calculate an ideal frame size, unless the manufacturer also provides the traditional centre-to-centre measurement in addition to the compact specification.

Choose a frame with the right seat-tube angle

The most important angle on a frame is the seat-tube angle. This is the angle made by the seat tube and an imaginary horizontal line. It significantly influences the saddle set-back position and therefore is of vital importance to determine the seat angle before buying the frame.

The seat-tube angle is related to the length of your upper leg (femur). A standard frame angle measures 72 to 75 degrees and allows a cyclist with an average-femur length to position the knee straight above the pedal axle with only small adjustments in fore and aft movement of the saddle. The longer your femur, the smaller the seat-tube angle and the farther back the saddle will have to be positioned.

Adjusting the contact points on your bike

On a bike, the weight of your body is supported at three locations:
• The pedals support your feet.

- The saddle supports your butt.
- The handlebars support your hands.

Ensure each is correctly positioned as described below.

Shoe cleats

Before you start to adjust other aspects of your position on the bike you first have to properly fit the shoe cleats. To maximize the efficiency of your 'ankling' and to avoid knee pain later on, the cleats should be adjusted so the ball of your foot is directly above the centre line of the pedal axle. This will allow you to realize optimal power transmission and the risk of the well-known burning feet sensation will considerably abate and in some cases even disappear completely.

Adjusting the saddle height

Once you have chosen the right frame and you've properly fitted the shoe cleats it's time to look at the height of the saddle as it is the most important aspect of positioning on your bike. The saddle height affects the muscle activity of your legs. If the saddle is placed too high you run the risk of over-stretching your muscles and when the saddle is placed too low the pressure on your quadriceps might become disproportionately high. The correct saddle height enables your muscles

to work optimally in the longitudinal reach and you will be able to maximize your power. You measure the saddle height from the heart of the bottom bracket to the upper part of the saddle in line with the seat post. To calculate your saddle height you have to know your inseam length. Your inseam length is measured as follows:

1. Stand straight up on your bare feet with your heels, back and head against a wall.
2. Position the inside of your feet approximately 15 to 20 centimetres (six to eight inches) apart.
3. Put a tube (eg a plastic bottle) with a diameter of three and a half to seven and a half centimetres (about one and a half to three inches) against your crotch, exerting the same pressure as your saddle would.
4. The edge of the tube should be horizontal and flush with the wall.
5. Ask a friend to draw a small line on the wall where the tube reaches its highest point.

The formula to measure the optimal saddle height = inseam length x 0.88.
Note: this saddle height calculation is based on Look Keo pedals and other pedals have a different stack height (check with manufacturers). This is the distance from the top of the

cleat to the centre of the pedal axle. The closer your foot is positioned to the axle the more efficiently power is transmitted to your bike. When you change pedals your foot might be closer to the axle. The lower the stack height, the lower the saddle height. As an example, 87.5 (inseam length) x 0.88 = 77cm saddle height with Look Keo pedals (stack height 17.1mm). When you then switch to, for example, Shimano SPD SL pedals (stack height 13.7mm) you should decrease your saddle height according to the difference in stack height between the two pedals. This is 17.1mm - 13.7mm = 3.4mm, giving a new saddle height of 76.6cm.

If you need to radically change your saddle height then make the adjustments gradually so your body has time to adapt! If you are currently used to a saddle height that is off by a lot, then adjust the saddle by 2 millimetres (a fraction of an inch) per week.

Fore and aft position of the saddle

The forward and backward adjustment (fore and aft position) of the saddle plays an important role as well. If your saddle is placed too far backwards it will result in an exaggerated lowering of your heel when your pedal reaches its maximum force angle at three o'clock (See Smooth pedal stroke

pages 42-45). If, on the other hand, the saddle is placed too far forwards your toes point down too much. This results in a loss of power and efficiency. (Note that many triathletes prefer a more forward position because it engages the muscles about to be used in the run). The following method allows you to properly adjust the fore and aft position.

First, get seated comfortably and click your cycling shoes (with properly mounted cleats) into the pedals while the crank arms and shoes are horizontal to the ground (ask a friend to check). Be sure the pressure in the front and rear tyres are equal and, even more importantly, the ground must be level!

Then drop a plumb line from the front of your forward kneecap. It should directly cross the forward pedal's axle. When the line drops in front or behind the pedal's axle you have to move the saddle forwards or backwards along its rails as needed.

The rails under the saddle have a margin of about 55 millimetres (2.2 inches) to move forwards and backwards. After any fore and aft adjustment you should recheck the saddle height. Moving the saddle forwards means you must slightly lower the saddle as well,

while moving the saddle backwards means you must slightly increase the saddle height. Your saddle should be level to support your full body weight and allow you to move around on the saddle when necessary. In almost no case is it a good idea to ride with a saddle that's tilted up at the front.

Too much upward tilt can result in pressure points. As you slide forward you are essentially pushing your most delicate parts into the nose of the saddle if it's up at the front which may lead to health problems later on. A downward-tilted saddle can make you slide forward while riding and put extra pressure on your arms, hands and knees, which can ultimately lead to injury. You can easily check the saddle's level by placing a spirit level along the longitudinal axis of the saddle.

Stem extension

The measurement that most influences your upper-body position is the combination of handlebar extension and top-tube length, or the so-called 'reach'. In a standard off-the-shelf frame the length of the top tube is correctly related to the length of the seat tube and correlates to the upper body measurements of a cyclist of average size who would need that frame size.

To determine a proper stem extension, place your hands in the drop position (or on the tops of the brake levers) while you are comfortably seated in your saddle with your elbows slightly bent (ground must be level!). In this position the front wheel's hub should then be obscured by the middle section of your handlebar. If proper top tube/stem length combination cannot be achieved with a 105-135 millimetres (4.1-5.3 inches) stem, try a larger frame.

It is clear that a correct aerodynamic position and a comfortable position of the torso do not always go hand in hand. Depending on your anatomy, flexibility and the distance you race, the reach could be longer for better aerodynamics and higher speeds, or it may need to be shorter for back or neck comfort and improved efficiency uphill. If your reach to the handlebar is wrong, use stem length to correct it, not fore/aft saddle position.

Stem height

Start with the top of the stem about four to five centimetres (about one and a half to two inches) below the top of the saddle. This should give you comfortable access to the handlebars. As time goes by you could lower the stem by another two to three centimetres (about an inch) to help your aerodynamic position. Going lower than this improves your aerodynamics but restrains breathing and your lower back or neck might start complaining. In general, the higher your stem, the better you will climb and the lower your stem, the more aerodynamic you will be. Most riders position their stems too low and rarely take advantage of the drop position of their handlebars.

Handlebar width

For a road bike, the handlebar width should correspond with the width of your shoulders. Handlebars that are too wide increase the frontal surface area and lead to a loss of aerodynamics. Contrary to general belief, narrow handlebars do not result in a loss of oxygen intake, but they lead to more nervous steering than wide handlebars and therefore the bike becomes less comfortable to ride.

Crank length

The great majority of cyclists use crank lengths of 170-175 millimetres (6.7-6.9 inches). Longer crank arms allow you to push larger gears at a lower cadence, while shorter arms promote high cadences with smaller gears. Sprinters, who need explosive power, are used to shorter cranks, while riders with good climbing abilities favour longer cranks.

Tri bikes

The information given in this section has been geared towards road bikes because if you are new to the sport and have entered a short race to find out if triathlon is for you, then a standard road bike, or indeed any roadworthy two-wheeler, will suffice. But if you intend on competing regularly and can afford to pay extra, then something more specific might be the answer.

When it comes to body position on the bike there is often a trade off between comfort and aerodynamics. At short distances you can sacrifice comfort for the aerodynamic position that generates the most power. Longer distances stretched out over the bars tend to weaken the core muscles, stress the lower back and reduce power output to a significant degree. Choose your bike with these factors in mind.

Road bikes have a seat-tube angle of about 72 to 75 degrees and put you in a more upright position. With the standard geometry, technical skills such as cornering, climbing and drafting are easier and allow for more control, especially at high speed. The design of the handlebars allows for quick switches from brake hoods to drops and facilitates short bursts of power when sprinting. Tri bikes have a seat-tube angle of 78

to 81 degrees and put the rider in a more forward position. This has the dual purpose of increasing aerodynamics and maintaining a position thought to be better for the muscles needed in running section to follow. Although these machines are designed specifically for triathlon, the combined elements of cost and the advanced handling skills needed, may make them a poor choice for a newcomer to triathlon.

You can modify a standard road bike to make it more tri specific by adding bolt-on aerobars. The only problem here, however, is the sharper angle created between the thigh and the upper torso as the rider adopts a more forward position. One solution is to push the saddle forward to relieve the severity of the stretch. Be aware though, that significant changes will alter the overall balance of the bike, making it less easier to control.

Shop around and decide which bike is right for you, based on your own needs and how much you can afford. Buy from a dealer who understands your needs and can give you advice regarding set-up. Every minor adjustment you can make to assist in the areas of power output, aerodynamics and comfort will have a positive and lasting effect on your overall performance.

Running

When it comes to equipment, running is one of the easiest sports around. After all, people have been running as long as man has existed – all that's needed is a safe, open space and you are away. The finest piece of equipment you'll ever have is your own body so always concentrate on that first and foremost. However, there are a number of items that can enhance your running experience and help improve your training and as you do not need much equipment it will not cost you a fortune to get properly kitted out.

Stopwatch

Although this is a pretty basic tool it is useful in helping you keep track of your running splits and when doing interval training. You do not need to spend a lot of money on this but you will find yourself using it for most runs.

Heart-rate monitor

The most important features you will use on a heart-rate monitor are those that measure your current heart rate, average heart rate and your highest and lowest heart rates during a run. These are all important for you to measure the intensity of workouts and follow your progress as a runner. The more advanced ones have a lot more features that you can upload to a computer and produce graphs and statistics of your runs. There are some reasonably priced monitors available that will provide you with all the basics.

GPS running watch

This is an optional tool and many elite athletes have successfully trained and competed in races and broken world records without such technology. Having said that, they can be useful and add fun to your running. A GPS watch (many are often just known by their trade name) can also be a great motivational tool and if you are a bit of a statistics freak then there is nothing better than getting home from a long run and checking your kilometre-by-kilometre splits. A watch will show the distance you have run, your speed, gradients you have climbed, as well as averages and other statistics. Once uploaded you can view all this information in graphs. This is a useful tool, as many runners tend to exaggerate or have wishful thinking about the distances they run. A slight word of warning: some runners get almost addicted to the statistics on their watch and can't even run a couple of metres without looking down at it. This will mean you can end up running as fast as you think you should be running, instead of listening to your body and adjusting your speed depending on how your body is responding to the workout that day.

Clothes

Running kit can really vary in price but you do not need to spend a lot of money. All you really need to run is a pair of shorts and a T-shirt, although there are certain situations, such as training in the dark or the wet where you should look at using other clothing. Bright colours (and lights) are crucial for your safety in bad light and there is a lot of dry-fit clothing that works well at drawing the moisture away from the body and keeping some warmth in when it is wet. Running jackets are also useful for the slower training runs on cold days and the high-quality ones are light, comfortable and waterproof, allowing an easy running style. They will also normally have some sort of reflector on them to help keep you visible. If you intend to wear a tri suit in the race make sure you get used to it in training at some point.

Running shoes

Good running shoes are essential. It doesn't matter what they look like, but it is vital they are the correct shoes for you and feel comfortable. You should get your running gait analyzed by an expert so the correct shoes are found for you. It cannot be overestimated how important this is, especially if you are going to be hitting the high-mileage training programmes. The correct shoes will also help you to avoid injury. Check out one of the elasticated/toggle lace options, which means you don't have to tie your laces and will speed up your transition.

technique
& tactics

// SHARPER // SMARTER // MORE EFFICIENT

The basics

Most of you will have come into triathlon from one of the three disciplines it incorporates – for most people this is running or cycling. You have some experience of racing in 'your own' sport, consider yourself to be fit and want to start stretching and testing yourself a bit further.

Then comes the crunch. Not only do you have to start relearning two other sports (most of us have had some experience of all three disciplines at some time, even if it was way back in our school days) but you have to discover how to combine all three and start treating them as one sport.

No matter how fit you consider yourself to be, you will benefit from improved technique in all areas of triathlon. A few simple technical improvements in your swimming, cycling and running will help shave valuable seconds and minutes off your race time but most importantly will harness your fitness and energy in the right way.

Sheer guts and determination can overcome poor technique to some extent (although more often than not this will lead to injuries) but good technique can achieve the same results – meaning you have your strength stored up for when you need it most.

Simply put, do you want to be an athlete who trains to the limit then falls over the line exhausted in a disappointing time or do you want to train smarter and smoother and see real results on race day?

Use this section to get the basics correct for your two 'weaker' disciplines, but also revisit your strongest discipline to look for any improvements you can make. Remember you now have to train across three disciplines, which means the time previously dedicated to your sport will be reduced. So, for instance, if you came into triathlon from a running background you may now find yourself out on the road only two to three times a week instead of five or more because of the time you need getting your swimming and cycling up to scratch. Good technique can counter this drop in quantity.

And there can be no better place to get things right than at the transitions. Progressing from the water to your bike and later from your wheels to your feet can make or break your race. It's not only the time you lose by fumbling around at transitions but the momentum you lose as a result. A nice, smooth transition that goes as planned, can act as a mental boost and keeps your mind focused on the real job at hand.

For most of us new to triathlon, swimming is the least favourite part of the race. Concentrate on a smooth stroke and getting your body position, leg kick, hand entry and breathing right and swimming, even in open water, needs hold no fears.

Cycling offers many opportunities to improve your technique so take time to look at all the aspects you will encounter, from hill climbing to downhills, to cornering to drafting (when allowed). Save a few seconds at every corner, every climb and every descent and your race times will tumble. Again, smoothness is everything, so work on your pedal stroke and eliminating the 'dead spots' (see pages 42-45) at the top and bottom of each pedal cycle, which waste so much time.

As you tire, an efficient technique becomes more and more important. As you enter the running phase of the triathlon, confidence in your technique will help you overcome fatigue and carry you home. Work on the small elements of technique during your running training and learn to listen to your body to see what works for you. Keeping your style loose and relaxed is the key, and it will hold you in good stead as you approach the final, gruelling part of your triathlon.

Swimming pool

1. Get into your own, steady pace and do not go chasing off in pursuit of the swimmer ahead of you.

2. It can be unnerving being surrounded by other swimmers. Keep relaxed and do not panic.

3. If you feel your heart rate rising too quickly then ease up and blow out the air in your lungs while your head's underwater before taking your next breath.

All triathlons start with the swim, but it's important to remember that they don't end there. To get the most from your performance on race day, plan well in advance and ensure that you have all the main points covered, from fuelling to equipment changes.

Before setting off, make a checklist of all the equipment you will need and tick each one off as you get it ready. You may think most items are obvious, like your bike and running shoes, but it's surprising what you can forget if it isn't written down.

When you get to the race site, find your allocated space in the transition area and rack your bike, then lay out all the items you need to complete the course on a towel alongside. Make sure you memorize the exact location of your bike in relation to the swim exit; this will help you stay focussed when you reach the transition area in the race.

Triathlon swims can be in a swimming pool or in open water. Your first triathlon experience is likely to be a sprint-distance race at a leisure centre, starting with a 400-metre swim in an indoor pool.

Swimmers go off in groups (size depends on race numbers but about 30-40 people per group). The whole group starts in the pool and goes off one by one with a few seconds interval between each swimmer. Your position in the line-up will be determined by your estimated finish time, with the faster swimmers starting in the first wave and the slowest last.

Warm up gently with either a brisk walk or a light jog, as you may not get the chance once you're in the water and the race begins. Practise deep breathing and relaxation exercises to prevent any last-minute nerves taking over and focus on your pacing strategy as you wait for the countdown.

For pool-based swims, you have the benefit of regulated water temperature, designated lanes and a level swimming surface. Factors like sighting and navigation don't apply as much, but you will need to be aware of other swimmers, both behind and in front of you. This can be strange at first but keep relaxed and don't let it panic you.

Set your own pace as soon as the gun goes and don't try to catch up with the swimmer in front as this will soon lead to exhaustion. If you feel your heart rate rising too quickly, ease up and focus on your technique, making sure to blow out all the air in your lungs while your head is underwater before you take the next breath in.

As you begin the last few lengths of your swim start to visualize the first transition, relaxing as much as possible in order to conserve energy for the next stage. In some leisure centres, the poolside is considerably higher than the waterline, and you will have to pull yourself out of the water. This is something you can practise in training to reduce the element of surprise and instil confidence for the race itself.

✓ Before you start make a checklist of everything you will need on race day.

✗ Don't try to memorize everything – you'll forget something important!

✓ Warm up gently before the start.

✗ Don't fight your nerves at the start or you will tense up.

✓ Keep a steady pace.

✗ Don't worry about chasing the person in front of you as soon as you get going.

✓ Visualize the transition period as you come to the end of your swim.

✗ Don't force your strokes towards the end – you need all your energy for the race ahead.

Open water

1 A mass start can be nerve-wracking. Ensure you stay warm, focussed and relaxed so you are ready to go.

2 A wetsuit is often obligatory for triathletes. Make sure you have had plenty of practise swimming in it so you are comfortable on race day.

3 Safety should be your first consideration. Unless you are among the fastest racers hang back at the start and give yourself some space.

Swimming in open water can come as a shock when you're used to the regulated safety of the pool. The conditions that you take for granted, such as set water temperature, good visibility and clear lane markings no longer apply. Add to this the stress of having perhaps hundreds of competitors around you, all heading in the same direction and you have some idea of the challenge involved.

Many European triathlon swims in open water require that you wear a wetsuit, as even in the summer season water temperatures can fluctuate. In order to acclimatize to swimming in a wetsuit as soon as possible, find a good supplier and get fitted out with a tri-specific wetsuit you can use both in training and on the day of competition. Wetsuits take some getting used to, so don't leave this aspect until the last minute and when you do venture into the water for the first time in a wetsuit make sure you have someone with you as a safety precaution.

At first, swimming in a wetsuit in open water may seem strange, due to the tightness of the material and the change of environment, but in time you will soon get used to it. You may find your breathing restricted at times, especially if the water is cold or you happen to be feeling particularly anxious, but if

this happens then ease up and let the natural buoyancy of the wetsuit support you until you feel confident enough to carry on.

The major difference between swimming in a pool and open water is navigation. In the pool, lanes are clearly marked and visibility is good, making it easy for you to get from one end to the other without too much difficulty. Open water has no such safeguards and requires you to constantly reassess your position in order to stay on course.

The problems of temperature changes, unpredictable weather conditions and flailing swimmers makes navigation even harder. As with all aspects of triathlon, the more you familiarize yourself in training the more confident you will be on the day of the race.

Be prepared to adapt your breathing during sea swims where sudden waves can catch you off guard. Practise breathing bilaterally rather than on one side only so you are ready for choppy waters. Lake and river surfaces tend to be flat, but the turbulence created by so many swimmers often makes the going rough in places.

The race swim course is marked out by a series of coloured buoys

and to reduce the risk of injury and confusion, safety officials are on hand to patrol the perimeters. But with so much activity in the water it is not always possible to see the marker buoys clearly and to ascertain your position. For this reason it is often more practical to find landmarks or other visible features you can use as aids to navigation.

In open water, good sighting will prevent you from drifting off course and help shave vital seconds off your swim time. As most of us don't live near the sea, or have access to a lake in which to adapt, the bulk of training may well be done in an indoor pool. This is fine as long as you practise the sighting technique and visualize the open water environment at regular intervals.

With standard front crawl your head is always aligned with your body to assist streamlining and breathing. Open water swimming requires that you raise your head every few strokes to sight landmarks or buoys and stay on course. Practise this technique as often as you can, adapting your swim stroke to incorporate your changed head position and altered breathing.

Get used to the feel of your wetsuit, in and out of the water, and try to get several open water swims in before the race, even if you have to travel some distance to do so. Be sure to practise the exit as you head for the transition area, making sure you can easily locate the zipper cord on the back of your wetsuit to assist a quick change.

Race day

The mass start of an Ironman is an amazing spectacle. With hundreds of bodies churning up the water at the sound of the gun, the sense of confusion can be overwhelming. Your first triathlon is unlikely to be on such a large scale, but if staged in open water it will contain similar elements you need to be aware of in order to prepare.

Your first consideration should always be safety. The fastest swimmers will all line up at the front in order to breakaway as early as possible, so unless you consider yourself fast enough to keep up with them, hang back. Even if you consider yourself a strong swimmer, for your first triathlon it is advisable to find a position on the outskirts and steer clear of the pack.

Keep warm while you are lining up and regulate your breathing. Listen carefully to the race organiser's announcement for details of any last-minute course changes

and for that all important message of good luck. As you wait for the countdown, pick out any features and landmarks to use for navigation and visualize the swim ahead.

As soon as the race is underway focus on bringing your breathing under control and avoid getting caught up in the pack. Don't use the swimmer in front for navigation, as he may be drifting off course. Stick to the fixed landmarks, coloured marker buoys or any features you picked out earlier and head for these.

Towards the end of the swim course start to think about the first transition. As your body has been horizontal for some time and your legs fairly static, circulation in the lower torso is often restricted. To increase flow kick your legs steadily, avoiding any sudden lunges that might raise your heart rate and heighten fatigue.

Swim as far as you can towards the shore before standing up, as running or wading through shallow water is extremely tiring and may cause you to stumble. As soon as you are on your feet, stay calm and head for dry land in a swift but controlled manner, focusing on transition and the next phase of the race ahead.

✓ Hang back at the start and find yourself some space.

✗ Don't get caught up in the crowd.

✓ Pick a landmark on the horizon to guide you in your navigation.

✗ Don't follow the swimmer in front – he may be heading in the wrong direction.

✓ Once racing, concentrate on your breathing and keeping your stroke smooth.

✗ Don't panic if you feel crowded.

✓ Towards the end of the swim increase your kicking speed to help circulation as you prepare to exit the water.

✗ Avoid sudden lunges that will increase your heart rate dramatically.

4 You will have to adapt your stroke technique when in open water by raising your head regularly to ensure you are still on course.

5 Brightly coloured buoys mark the course but it is better to pick out a landmark before you start and keep swimming towards that.

6 You will need to adapt your breathing technique in choppy water. Learn to breathe bilaterally.

The stroke

1 Get your elbows out of the water first – this lets you stretch further for maximum pull.

2 Put in a complete 90-degree head turn for each breath so you don't swallow water.

3 When starting out adopt a breathing pattern you are comfortable with but do not feel afraid to change it during a race.

While there are certainly no restrictions to the swimming stroke you use in a triathlon, almost everyone uses freestyle (although some first-timers and those wanting a breather sometimes use breaststroke). Remember that you may need to adapt your technique when swimming in open water (see pages 32-35).

Body position

Head: your head should be positioned with your eyes looking at approximately 45 degrees to the water's surface with the water hitting the crown of your head. It is important your head remains still between breathing to help maintain your body's streamlined position.

Head position during breathing: your head should turn 90 degrees when you are breathing. It is important to make sure your head turns as little as possible so that you minimize the disturbance to your body's streamlined position. Your head rotation will be assisted by your upper body's rotation; timing is key in ensuring your head turns as your shoulders rotate.

Hips and upper body: your shoulders should rotate to help keep the stroke long and to ensure that your body is streamlined at all times. As your hand enters the water

one shoulder will drop while your other shoulder will rotate in the opposite direction. Your shoulders should rotate to around 45 degrees to the surface of the water, which will reduce the surface area of your body as it travels through the water. Your hips should follow through the rotation of your shoulders.

Leg kick

The freestyle leg kick is important

because it helps you to maintain your body's position in the water as well as aiding your forward propulsion. A strong leg kick will help you to maintain your body's position at the surface of the water. Aim for a relaxed and economical leg kick that won't tire your legs for the cycling section.

A six-beat kick is commonly used by swimmers, which means six kicks to every two arm strokes or one complete arm cycle. Your legs should be kept long with minimal knee flexion, with the kick coming from your hip and your ankles loose with toes pointed.

Hand entry

Your hand should be rotated to a 45-degree angle as it enters the water with your finger tips entering before any other part of the hand. By entering the water with your hands at this angle they will be in the position to start the out sweep at the start of the pull.

✓ Breathe every two or more strokes.

✗ Don't try to breathe on every stroke – it wastes momentum.

✓ Breathe to the side and fully turn your head to maximize oxygen intake.

✗ Don't try to get your head fully out of the water when breathing.

✓ Do let your fingertips enter the water first on the pull stroke.

✗ Don't let your hands hit the water close to your head.

✓ Stretch your arms as fully as possible on the pull stroke.

✗ Don't kick from the knee – kick from the hip.

Your hand should enter as far from your head as possible to help ensure you have a long stroke.

Arms

Once your hand has entered the water, try to maintain a high elbow during the pull phase of the stroke. Your arms should start sweeping in an outward and downward direction. Then pull inwards and upwards just before the stroke pushes backwards, with your fingers exiting past the hip.

As your arm exits the water your elbow should be kept high and your hand close to your body as your other arm starts the pull phase. As your arm recovers over the water your elbow should be kept high with your fingers close to the water's surface as your arm stretches out over the water for a long hand entry.

Breathing

Swimmers have used different breathing patterns for freestyle swimming over the years, such as every two, three or four strokes and also combinations such as 2-2-3 and 4-4-2.

The most common breathing pattern is every three strokes. This is known as bilateral breathing, which ensures

regular oxygen intake without breaking your body's streamlined position too often to breathe. Breathing every two strokes will mean the stroke's streamlined position is broken more frequently, whereas when breathing every four or five strokes the stroke is kept streamlined for more of the swim but you will oxygenate less frequently.

When starting out or if you are still building up strength in swimming, you should adopt a breathing pattern you feel comfortable with and not try to emulate top swimmers (who can breathe as little as every five or six strokes in a 400-metre race). Even if you start out with a plan for your breathing pattern do not be afraid to change it during a race or training if you feel you need to.

If you haven't swum for a long time you will need to practise your breathing during training, so stop every 25 metres and fully fill your lungs before setting off again. Practise this until you feel confident enough to increase the distance to 50 metres and so on.

4 Keep the stroke long and efficient by rotating your shoulders and your hips will follow.

5 Use a six-beat freestyle kick – that is six kicks for one complete arm cycle.

6 Keep your head at 45 degrees to the surface to reduce drag and to maintain momentum.

Transition one – swim to bike

1 Memorize the sequence of events you will need to run through at the transition to reduce anxiety on race day.

2 Place a towel beside your bike and lay out the items you will need so they are close to hand when you get out of the water.

3 Ensure you do up the strap on your helmet before riding. It is best to hook your helmet upturned on handlebars with the straps hanging down.

The purpose of transition is to change clothing and equipment, refuel and head out onto the next phase of the course. To do this efficiently you need to ensure that all your kit is laid out in the required order at your allocated bike space before the start of the race.

The swim-to-bike transition can often be the most confusing, especially if it's your first race and fatigue has set in. Much of the anxiety can be reduced if you memorize the sequence of events beforehand and go through it regularly in training.

On race day each competitor racks his bike by hooking the saddle over a long length of horizontal tubing. To facilitate a quick getaway, make sure your bike faces out in a pre-selected easy gear, with your safety helmet laid across the handlebars with the straps hanging down.

Experienced triathletes often leave their cycling shoes clipped into the pedals before the race, but for a relative newcomer this is not advisable. If you have not used clip-in shoes before, make sure you get used to them during training

Lay a towel beside your bike on the opposite side to your chain crank

and put your cycling shoes down, making sure you loosen any Velcro straps. Sprinkle talcum powder inside your shoes and put a dab of petroleum jelly on the heel spur, and if you choose to wear socks, leave them inside your shoes where you can access them quickly when you exit the swim.

You should practise the routine of the transition in training. Set up your bike in a garage space or driveway and go through the sequence as it would happen on race day.

Get used to the feeling of cycling in wet clothing by taking a bath or shower in your tri suit and heading out on the bike. If your race starts in open water, find a suitable training location and set up a makeshift transition area. Ask a friend to look after your bike while you practise the swim exit and follow this by a short ride to get your body used to the feeling of the changeover from the water.

Wetsuits can be awkward to remove, especially when you are fatigued from the swim and surrounded by the frantic activity of other competitors. From a standing position, strip to the waist first, then peel the suit down over your legs and pull your feet free.

Have a full drinks bottle mounted on your bike so you can hydrate as soon as possible. On longer training rides, particularly in hot weather, it is wise to take more than one bottle with you and to drink regularly. Consume any power gels you wish to take with water only, as mixing them with sports drinks can cause stomach upsets and prevent digestion.

✓ Exit the swim and locate your bike. Remove your goggles, swim cap and wetsuit (if applicable) and leave them in the space allocated for your kit.

✓ Change into shorts (and socks if you wish to wear them) and slip into your cycling shoes, ensuring the Velcro flaps are secure. Put your bike helmet on and do up the straps, as failure to do so will incur a penalty.

✓ Ensure your race number is attached and clearly visible on the back of your top, and that you have any gels and drinks bottles with you.

✓ Unhook your bike and walk/jog to the mount line.

Smooth pedal stroke

1 Concentrate on 'pulling up' during the third and fourth quadrants of the stroke (from six to 12 o'clock), lifting your heel for extra pull.

2 Concentrate on 'pushing down' during the first quadrant of the stroke (from 12 to three o'clock).

3 Aim to move through the dead spots of the pedal cycle – 12 o'clock and six o'clock – as smoothly as possible.

A smooth pedal stroke is a critical aspect of the forward driving of your bike. Imagine the difference between an exhausted cyclist hitting his pedals as if he's hammering them down and the powerful cyclist who caresses his pedals by turning them around smoothly and forcefully. The difference in pedalling efficiency is enormous. In the history of professional cycling we have seen great cyclists successfully applying different pedalling techniques.

Jacques Anquetil became famous not only because of his achievements but also as the cyclist who set the benchmark for pedalling efficiency. Anquetil had a unique pedalling style, which held many secrets. He did biomechanically what the best engineers have tried in vain to do by mechanical means, which was to eliminate the entire dead spot area of the pedal stroke thanks to a phenomenal use of his ankles. His pedalling technique allowed him to extend the effective, profitable phase of his pedalling and therefore decreasing the force peak of each pedal stroke.

Engineers since have been studying the biomechanical and physical factors involved in pedalling. Very few, though, have been able to find a mechanical solution by developing a product that improves the pedalling efficiency.

Biomechanists studying the pedalling efficiency look at the different forces a cyclist applies on the pedals to identify and teach pedalling technique. They differentiate two different force components that influence the pedalling efficiency.

The first component is the tangential force component that transmits rotational force to the crank arm and is thus a component of effective force as it is powering the bike ahead.

The second component, the radial force component, acts parallel to the crank arm along the surface of the pedal and therefore only tends to alter the shape by 'lengthening' or even 'deforming' the crank arm and, producing no rotary force, which represents an ineffective force component.

With regard to pedalling technique, the extent to which these two forces are applied on the pedals will result in a more (or less) efficient pedal stroke. Applying more tangential force to the crank and reducing the radial force is the most effective way to increase your pedalling efficiency. The result is increased torque, which is the product of the tangential force component and the crank-arm length.

Although you won't notice it while riding, the applied force on the pedal throughout the pedal stroke changes continuously, both in intensity and direction. A pedal stroke consists of four quadrants: the first quadrant downward and forward, the second downward and backward, the third upward and backward, and the fourth quadrant upward and forward returning to the starting point.

During the pedal stroke you will be confronted with the so-called 'dead spot', or the top dead centre of the pedal stroke. Analysis with force-measuring devices have showed that when the pedals are on the top with the cranks in a vertical position, the applied force on the pedal is close to zero. During the first quadrant, after going through the dead top centre, you gradually increase your force output until the crank arm reaches the three o'clock position. At this point you attain the peak force of the pedal stroke.

In the second quadrant, from the three o'clock position until the dead bottom centre of the pedal rotation, the force on the pedal is decreasing significantly. During the third and fourth quadrants (from six to 12 o'clock) of the stroke the weight of your foot and leg apply a negative force, which is slowing down the upward movement of the pedals and thus causing a counter torque.

But what can you do to improve your pedalling? The answer is not simple because the complex web of physical and mechanical variables makes it difficult for cyclists, coaches, manufacturers and scientists to apply biomechanics to cycling. But there are certain factors that are adjustable and therefore can help improve your performance and pedalling efficiency.

The muscles you use to pedal and your ankle movement are interrelated, with adjustable mechanical factors like the frame geometry, saddle height, crank length, type of pedals, foot position, type of chain rings (circular or non-circular) etc. A proper bike fit, along with correct cleat positioning is essential to optimizing the efficiency of your pedal stroke (see The basics on pages 18-22).

To optimize your pedal efficiency you need to get the maximum benefit from your ankle movement. Optimal ankle movement or 'ankling' consists of progressively pushing down through the top

of your stroke and pulling up at the bottom. The action involves a lowering of the heel as the downward force of the pedals takes place and a lifting of the heel as the pedal begins the upward movement of its revolution.

The key point of ankling is to always stay focused on the leverage of your crank arms by the upward pulling of the pedals during the recovery phase of the pedal motion. This technique enables the application of constant pressure upon the pedals throughout the revolution, eliminating, to a certain extent, the dead spots at the upper and lower points of the cycle.

The result is a pedal stroke that requires less peak muscle contraction, which spreads the load over the muscles (engaging more calf muscles) and promoting a smooth, efficient style. You will be able to produce more power with less difficulty. This technique can be applied during climbing with low-rotation speed. However, during high-speed sections with high cadences riders cannot think about individual strokes and revert to what comes naturally to them.

Typically cyclists will apply different ankle movements while pedalling. Depending on your flexibility and

basic biomechanics, you may use a high heel action and/or a low heel action. Also your speed and cadence have a large influence: the faster your cadence, the more difficult it will be to keep control over your pedalling technique. The downwards force on the pedals and the muscle contraction will be so quick in a sprint at 140 RPM that you won't be able to manage your pedalling technique.

You'll notice that while sprinting on the flat with such a high cadence your toes tend to point down significantly. When you're spinning (pedalling fast with little resistance) you don't need to generate much power and your foot favours the least possible movement at the ankle, thus maintaining a vertical angle to your lower leg. But as you pedal more slowly, perhaps needing more power for a climb or to push through a headwind, modifying the angle of your foot at various points of the pedal stroke can increase your power. The low heel technique is important in hill climbing while sitting back on the saddle and you'll notice an improvement in your climbing abilities once you master this technique.

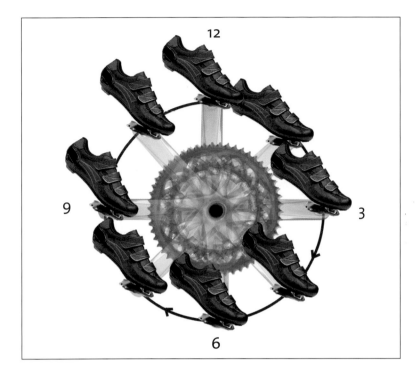

This illustrates the ideal ankling technique for **riding on the flat** (90+ RPM). Notice the strong 'unrolling' motion between three and six o'clock and the higher ankle/heel during the complete pedal stroke compared to the technique for riding uphill. Toes should be pointed more downwards and this effect will be even more visible when increasing your cadence. This is an automatic tendency so don't try to force your natural ankle movement. You may end up injuring yourself if you attempt to change the natural heel height of your pedal stroke. Remember: you should try to develop ankling within the bounds of your basic pedalling movement, always respecting your natural abilities.

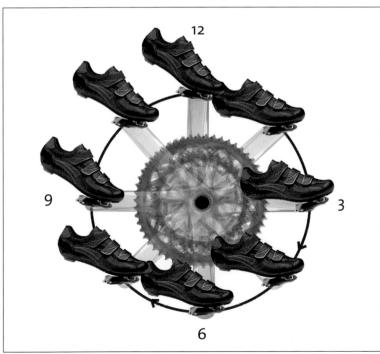

This illustrates the ideal ankling technique for **riding uphill** (ie 60-90 RPM). The ankling pattern will vary from an almost horizontal foot position at one o'clock to slightly heel down at three o'clock. The heel down lowering should then reduce progressively until your pedal reaches the lowest position at six o'clock and gets the toes back by the time the pedal reaches the five o'clock position. When the pedal reaches the upstroke (from six o'clock to 12 o'clock) of the pedal motion (the so-called recovery phase) your toes should slightly point downwards and your heel move up with a maximum toes-down position at eight o'clock of the pedal stroke.

Drafting

1 Drafting will save you up to 20 to 30 per cent of your energy. Tuck in close to benefit.

2 Ride at a comfortable distance from others when first riding in a group. About 50cm to 70cm (20in to 28in) is a good starting point.

3 Focus on the group as a whole rather than only on the rider in front of you.

Drafting is when you ride behind another rider or in a group of riders to get the benefit of the reduced airflow, so that you are working less and conserving energy for later in the race. Essentially you are getting a 20 to 30 per cent advantage of drafting the riders in front of you as compared to when you are riding alone or in the front of a group. If you are in a bigger group, your benefit can be even greater than this.

You should be aware that drafting when cycling is only permitted in some triathlons so always check beforehand or risk being penalised. Drafting is also looked down on by some racers as not being 'pure'. However, it is a useful tool, even if it is only used in training, so it should not be ignored by triathletes.

To get comfortable with riding in groups, start by riding in a small group first. A group of five or six people is ideal to learn the basic techniques needed when riding in a group. Start by maintaining a distance from the other cyclists that makes you feel comfortable. When you are not acquainted with riding in a group this distance can mean keeping your front wheel anywhere from 50 to 70 centimetres (20 to 28 inches) from the rear wheel of the rider immediately in front of you.

The distance from your shoulders to the shoulders of those either side of you will be about the same to start with, but again, use the 'comfortable' rule. Over time, as your confidence and technique improves, this distance can get closer. Professional cyclists can ride at high speeds while rubbing shoulders and almost touching the wheel of the cyclist in front of them, but this takes a rare talent and years of practise.

What you need to learn to do is to be able to gauge the distance of the wheel in front of you by focusing on the rider(s) beyond the bike that is/are riding ahead of you. It is the same as when driving a car – you judge the position of your vehicle by looking forwards and using your peripheral vision, not focusing only on the front of your car. In this way you are going to learn where your bike is in relation to the other riders in the group.

You should always avoid staring down at the wheel right in front of you, or your own wheel, because that can be very dangerous. You need to be looking ahead of you. Another tip, especially when you start riding closer to the other riders and closing the gap, is to always ride slightly to the left or the right side of the wheel

of the person in front of you and not follow in a direct straight line. In that way you have the ability to move gently to either side according to the slight movements of the other rider.

✓ Get close to the rider in front of you to benefit from drafting.

✗ Not too close to avoid accidents.

✓ Keep your eyes looking forward and use your peripheral vision.

✗ Don't look down at your front wheel.

✓ Practise riding in a small group to start with until you gain in confidence.

✗ Don't move into bigger groups until you have experience.

Hill climbing

1 Approach the hills as a challenge not a problem and your motivation levels will rise.

2 When riding out of the saddle keep centred so the power is pushing down through the pedals and don't pull hard on the handlebars.

3 Before you hit the steepest part of the climb make sure you have already set up your chosen gear.

Most people see a climb as a huge obstacle and their motivation drops when they look up. But hills are an integral part of training and racing and you will need to learn to embrace them with confidence if you want to start reducing your race times. Hill climbing may never become your favourite part of cycling but with good technique, mental approach and fitness levels you will discover there is nothing to fear from a hill or mountain climb. You will even start to enjoy the challenge over time and when a climb becomes a challenge your motivation levels to take on the climb will rise as you approach it.

As you approach the hill always prepare your gears before you hit the steepest grades. Obviously if the climb starts with a low gradient you can enter it in higher gears and adjust your gears gradually as the gradient increases. But do not attack the steepest part of a climb with a big gear that results in your pedal cadence grinding to a halt – maintain your momentum and keep turning your legs.

When you are on the flat you will have to shift to the smaller ring in the front before the transition to the hill. As you shift and allow the chain to drop to the smaller ring, continue pedalling but gently

relieve the pressure on the pedals so the chain doesn't drop off onto the inside. Relieving this pressure is very difficult if you are struggling in a high gear on a steep gradient because of the pressure the chain is under and you may be forced to come to a virtual standstill to be able to relieve that pressure enough to change to the correct gear. This may sound like a beginner's mistake but even professionals sometimes find themselves facing a long, steep climb from a standing start because of a poor gear change. There is nothing worse than having to dismount on a climb and having

to turn your pedals manually to change to the correct gear.

Assuming you have shifted successfully going into the hill, you must then select the appropriate gear from the cassette for the gradient of the hill. Riding uphill is all about managing your effort and not your speed so consider that when choosing your gear. It's important to get to the top of the climb within your capabilities rather than trying to force yourself into keeping up a certain speed you may not be able to maintain. If you are approaching the hill at a high speed you clearly shouldn't expect to maintain this high speed until the top of the hill. So keep focusing on managing your effort, not your speed. This will help you pace yourself up the hill. When you use a heart-rate monitor or a device that measures your wattage output you can control your effort more accurately.

Don't attempt to win points by conquering a hill in a high gear – it is more effective to maintain a higher pedal cadence in a lower gear. One of the reasons why Lance Armstrong became a Tour de France champion is because he was able to spin his legs with a high cadence with lower gears.

An optimal pedal cadence to maintain speed and for maximum energy efficiency depends on the abilities and fitness of each individual rider but is around 60-90 RPM. Any lower than 60 RPM and you are significantly increasing the force (and energy) you are applying to each pedal stroke and any higher than 90 RPM you are increasing your heart rate (and using your energy) without any associated benefit.

Another important part of hill climbing is the positioning of your hands on the handlebar. Generally, the tops of the handlebar are used

for riding uphill, especially if you are at the front of a group or if you are riding alone, as this will naturally force you to straighten up, therefore opening up your lungs and giving you more air for the climb. As you climb you must relax your body and breathe steadily. Tensing up will affect your breathing patterns.

If you are riding uphill in the middle of a group then place your hands on the shifters as this allows you to access your gears and brakes if you need to react to a change in the speed or rhythm of the group. Another advantage of placing your hands on the shifters is that this is the right position for when you decide to get out of the saddle. If the hill is getting steep this will give you leverage, allowing you to transmit more power on the pedals as you move the handlebars slightly to the left and to the right.

Avoid leaning forward to keep your power driving down the centre of the bike through the pedals. Riding out of the saddle will increase your heart rate and give you more power but use this sparingly to burst through steep sections or to change the working muscles briefly.

Your foot position is also an important aspect when you

are climbing. For most people, the foot should be flat when the crank position is horizontal and that foot position should be maintained throughout the pedal stroke. You shouldn't change the flexion between your foot and your shin too much. Some people have a tendency to ride with their toes down (like the legendary cyclist Jacques Anquetil), others with the heel down and the toes up (like Eddy Merckx), but the best position for most people is flat. Whatever your natural tendency or preference, try to keep that same angle throughout your pedal stroke.

✓ See a hill as a challenge.

✗ Do not fear a hill.

✓ Ride at a pedal cadence of 60-90 RPM.

✗ Avoid gears that are too low for this range.

✓ Relax your body as you climb.

✗ Don't tense up or your breathing will be affected.

✓ Stay centred over the bike when out of the saddle.

✗ Avoid leaning forward.

4 When riding in a group put your hands on the shifters so you can manoeuvre the bike and brake quickly if needed.

5 Position your hands on top of the handlebars if you have space to ride, such as when you are leading a group or riding alone.

6 The key to climbing is to manage your effort not your speed. Don't get fixated on maintaining a particular speed.

Cornering

| **1** Concentrate on keeping your weight centred through the bike. | **2** Push forward with your inside hand as you enter the turn. | **3** Push down on your outside pedal as you enter the turn. |

Steering around a corner is not simply a matter of turning the handlebars. This technique is fine when used at low speeds but when professionals or advanced riders think about steering a bike they will talk of another technique: the counter-steering method.

This is the technique you need to master when cornering on a downhill stretch at higher speeds or riding fast in a group. At a high speed you can't just steer through a turn because your bike will skip out and you will not be able to lean into it.

So, as you increase your speeds on your bike, you must use the method of counter steering. As you start to approach a turn, let's say a right turn, you need to turn your outside pedal down (the left pedal in this case). You then apply pressure with your foot on your outside pedal and gently push forward with your inside hand (in this case your right hand).

This turns the handlebars very slightly in the opposite direction and causes your bike to create the necessary lean to initiate the turn. Avoid putting too much pressure on your handlebars with your hands as you will be forcing it and this will cause you to slip, especially during wet weather conditions. Trust the technique to corner you successfully.

Counter steering allows your bike to fall into position naturally and to get into the correct lean position to make the turn. While you push your outside pedal down you have to think about your core and your weight on the saddle, concentrating on driving straight through the bike and the bottom bracket through to the ground. It's important to stay focused on maintaining the weight of your body through the centre. Anyone who has been skiing may recognize this technique, as keeping your weight through the centre of the body is similar for keeping control and balance.

As you approach a corner you need to select the line that allows you to maintain speed as much as possible. The line should take you from the outside of the corner as you approach, then to the inside on its apex and swinging back to the outside again as you leave the corner.

Obviously, when riding at low speed, such as when you are climbing a hill, the counter-steering method is not applicable.

✔ Use the counter-steering method to corner at speeds.

✘ Do not simply turn the handlebars.

✔ Push down on your outside pedal.

✘ Don't allow your inside pedal to drift downwards.

✔ Push your inside hand slightly forward to create the turn.

✘ Don't force the movement on the handlebars.

✔ Choose your line as you approach the corner.

✘ Don't allow your weight to be shifted forward.

Downhill

1 Build your confidence slowly when increasing your downhill speed.

2 Keep your hands on the drops during the descent so you are more able to react if there is a problem ahead.

3 Adopt a streamlined position to reduce wind resistance.

There are two types of downhill riding you need to master: straight and cornering. You need a good technique in the first instance but after that it is a matter of being stronger than your fear. But that does not mean taking undue risks.

Build your confidence and your speed slowly as you learn to trust the techniques for going downhill at speed. The fastest downhill professional cyclists push themselves to the very edge, using every millimetre of the road to maximize their speed. It is not necessary to take your downhill racing to such extremes but learning how to race effectively at speed will be an important part of improving your times and your position in your races.

When cycling downhill in a straight line or a very gradual bend you can adopt a more streamlined position to reduce wind resistance and increase your speed. This requires you to lower your back, shoulders and head into a more horizontal position. This will cause your back to stretch out and may require you to slide back in your seat slightly.

You may have seen some professional cyclists descending with their hands almost together, centred on the top of the handlebars to

minimize the wind resistance. This is something only advanced cyclists attempt (and then, not even all of them). The time-saving advantage is minimal and reduces your ability to react if there is a problem on the road ahead such as a stone or a hole.

Keep your hands on your drops so they are close to the shifters. Certainly do not attempt to copy the crazy downhillers who descend with their stomach balanced on the saddle and their eyes peering just over the handlebars as if they are riding a rocket!

When cornering downhill at speed you will almost automatically need to use the counter-steering method (see pages 52-53). The key point is to always focus on keeping your body weight driving through the centre of the bike.

This is important because on a downhill your body weight will be naturally pitched forwards unless you concentrate on keeping it back and centred. On extreme downhills you may have seen professionals shifting backwards in their saddle as they approach a corner, which is them ensuring their weight is centred (as well as a way of increasing braking efficiency). Remember, the steepness of the downhill and the resulting speed you enter into a corner determines how much you will be pitched forward and therefore how much adjustment you will need to make.

You should be aware that if you go too far back your rear tyre might start to slip. Gradually, with experience, you will learn to feel the right amount of adjustment needed to stay centred.

Braking into a corner, because of the pressure applied to the front wheel, will also cause your body to be pitched forward, so concentrate on applying even pressure to both brakes. Too much pressure on the front brake increases the chance of sliding, especially during the wet weather.

Before taking a sharp corner apply your brakes early enough to ensure you enter the corner at a speed that allows you to take that corner without braking again. Because you are leaning into the bend your tyres' contact with the road is reduced and therefore braking at this time is more likely to cause you to slide away. Again, slowly build

your confidence as you gradually learn the correct speed at which to enter a corner without the need to brake as you take it.

Remember, although it is unlikely that any two corners in the world are exactly the same, the more corners you take successfully and the faster you are able to take them at, the more you will build your confidence. Downhill speed and downhill cornering is a matter of trial and error – try to use trial and not error because error can be a very painful experience

when you are travelling on two wheels at 50 kph (31 mph).

Finally, consider that in hilly and mountainous environments you will frequently encounter lower temperatures. Practise putting on a wind jacket as you are cycling and get into the habit of putting it on as you are about to enter the descent. Over time you can become quite proficient at putting on your jacket quickly (and taking it off when you have completed your descent). Obviously you can skip this if the temperatures are soaring!

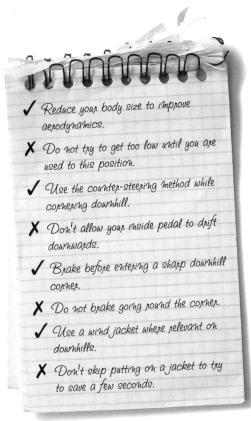

✓ Reduce your body size to improve aerodynamics.

✗ Do not try to get too low until you are used to this position.

✓ Use the counter-steering method while cornering downhill.

✗ Don't allow your inside pedal to drift downwards.

✓ Brake before entering a sharp downhill corner.

✗ Do not brake going round the corner.

✓ Use a wind jacket where relevant on downhills.

✗ Don't skip putting on a jacket to try to save a few seconds.

4 Concentrate on keeping centred over your bike as entering a bend downhill will naturally pitch you forward.

5 Apply your brakes before entering a sharp bend not during the turn.

6 Apply both brakes evenly when cycling downhill as too much pressure on the front increases the chance of sliding.

Transition two – bike to run

1 Your legs can be loose and ready for the run if you have dropped down to an easier gear to help increase blood flow at the end of the cycle.

2 Conserve your energy at the start of the run and do not be tempted to chase the runner in front.

3 Always make sure you have a peaked cap with your equipment in the transition area – you will need it in sunny weather.

The run section of a triathlon is the toughest of all the disciplines and soon reveals whether your preparation has paid off. Many experienced runners come into the sport expecting to excel in the final third, only to find their leg muscles have been drained on the bike. The best way to avoid this is by combining the two disciplines in training and getting used to the changeover.

Cyclists often use weight training to strengthen their leg muscles, but by the end of the bike leg

during a triathlon, it is often the core muscles that are called upon to absorb most of the shock. Avoid pushing big gears on the bike and aim instead for a smooth pedal stroke with a fairly high cadence that brings you into transition with energy to spare.

As you approach transition, change into an easier gear and spin your legs to increase blood flow and ease stiff muscles. You may wish to loosen the straps to your cycling shoes to assist a faster transition, but if you are inexperienced it is advisable to keep them fastened until you have racked your bike.

At the end of the bike leg you will be required to dismount and walk/jog to the transition area. Practise this in training, using the end of a driveway as the dismount line and get used to the feel of running alongside your bike. Take care to step off on the side opposite the crank to avoid catching the chain and causing an injury.

As soon as you have racked your bike, focus on the things you will need for the run and go through the sequence as calmly as you can. If you wish to use energy gels or power bars, put them inside your

running shoes before the race, and keep a full drinks bottle alongside so you can hydrate as soon as you are in transition.

In extremely hot weather you will need a light hat with a peak to keep the sun off your head, so have this ready to hand in the transition area as well. Aid stations will provide water, and in longer distance races sports drinks, but you may wish to take your own to rehydrate as soon as possible.

When you exit the transition area and head out onto the run, aim to bring your heart rate down and settle into a pace you feel you can sustain until the finish line. The first few minutes are vital for focusing on your breathing and running form, so don't be tempted to chase the runner in front; conserve your energy instead.

✓ Dismount at the line and walk/jog with your bike to the transition area. Keep your helmet on and the straps done up until you get to your allocated space as failure to do so will incur a penalty.

✓ Rack your bike and take off your helmet. Make any necessary kit changes, ensuring that your race number is attached to the back of your top and is clearly visible.

✓ Change into your running shoes.

✓ Take any gels or drinks you may need with you and follow the signs for the run course.

Upper body

1 Maintain a tall posture, keeping your shoulders directly above your hips as if there is a straight line drawn between the two pointing directly up.

2 Arms should swing gently backwards and forwards.

3 Keep hands relaxed as if you are holding a piece of paper between your thumb and first finger.

There is no doubt most of the strength work for endurance runners is done in the lower body. Having said that, you will need a strong core to prevent injury, while in the shorter distances a good arm action can help to propel your body forwards faster.

You should keep your upper body relaxed when running. Keep your head still but without tension in your neck. Your eye line should be focused gently along the horizon (about 20-30 metres ahead of you). Keep your face and, in particular, your jaw relaxed.

✓ Keep your face relaxed.

✗ Do not tense up and hold your jaw in a fixed position.

✓ Keep your arms swinging gently forwards and backwards.

✗ Don't have any lateral movement.

✓ Keep your pelvic floor muscles gently engaged.

✗ Do not clench your hands.

✓ Keep your body tall over your hips.

✗ Do not lean forward.

Keep your shoulders relaxed (resist tensing up and pushing them towards your ears) and your upper body lifted nice and tall above the hips, so as not to restrict breathing. Try not to bend forwards from the hips or sink into the hips, as both can cause lower back pain.

Your arms should be held at a 90-degree angle with your hands held in a soft fist with your thumb gently resting on your forefingers. Avoid holding a clenched fist as the tension will spread through the whole upper body. A good way to relax this area is to imagine you are gently holding a thin piece of paper between your thumb and first finger. The movement of your arms should be forwards and backwards with no lateral movement; any side movement will cause a very uneconomical running action.

To prevent injury it is also worth engaging your pelvic floor muscles (this is best described as the muscle group which you use to stop yourself going to the toilet). Gently squeeze these muscles (around 30 per cent effort), as this will help activate your core muscles which will in turn support your back and reduce the risk of injury. Using your pelvic floor muscles is definitely one

to practise in your core and cross-training sessions.

As you can see, the key to correct technique in the upper body is to relax and not carry tension. Many runners, in their determination to go quicker, keep their upper body very stiff, but this tension is energy sapping and unproductive. As with most of your running form, practice makes perfect. So, when you are out training it is worth spending a couple of sessions really focusing on your upper body and maintaining a smooth, easy, relaxed movement.

It is worth noting that many fast runners break technique rules, notably with the upper body. The distinctive running style of marathon runner Paula Radcliffe, whose head bobs about, clearly isn't from the running textbook. Coaches have almost certainly tried to prevent this head movement in the past, but forcing a technique that is supposed to help you run faster can sometimes cause a lot of tension and actually have the opposite effect. The most important thing is to keep relaxed and have a smooth, easy style.

Lower body

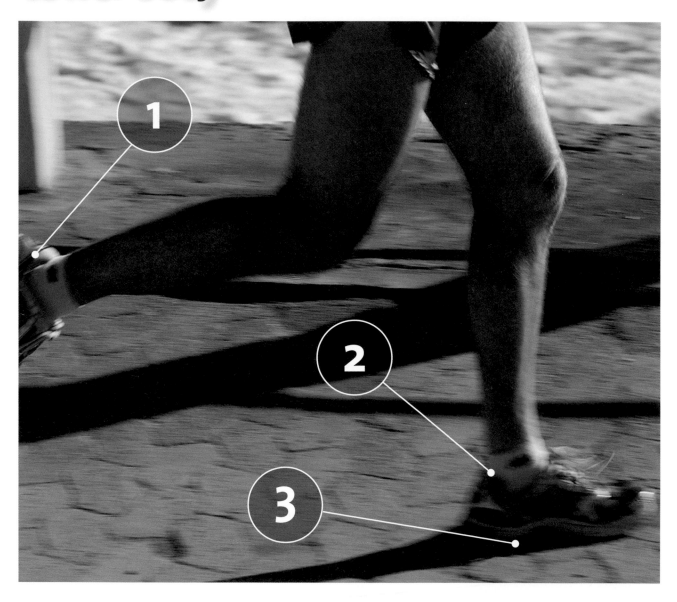

1 Kick your heel up to your backside.

2 Don't allow your ankle or knee joints to roll too far in or out.

3 Concentrate on having minimal contact time with the surface of the ground.

The work the lower body performs in endurance runs is immense. Therefore, the more economical your action is, the less energy you will expend, and the less chance there is of incurring an injury. Your leg action or running gait can be very hard to change, and you will find that most runners will revert to type. The more you run the more you will naturally find yourself become smoother in your action and covering greater distances with less effort. However, there are some fundamentals which everyone should take notice of.

✓ Kick your heel up towards your backside.

✗ Don't have a high knee lift.

✓ Wear the correct footwear to avoid injury.

✗ Watch out for over-pronating or supinating.

✓ Aim for minimal contact time with the ground.

✗ Don't place your foot down heavily.

✓ Practise your running form in training runs.

✗ Don't feel tension in your running form.

It's obviously difficult to look at your own running form but it's important you can see your own style because you will be immediately be able to pick up some pointers for improvement. The ideal way to do this is to get a friend to film you as you run. If you can't arrange this then you can see your style by running on a treadmill in front of a mirror or alternatively simply go running on a sunny day and look down at the shape and movement of your shadow.

Your back heel should kick up towards your backside. This will maximize the use of your hamstrings and glutes and will also propel your leg forward. Note, this running action is different from that of sprinters who bring their knees up high in front of the body. For most longer distance races the back heel will not need to kick too high, but even a small amount of backlift towards your backside will give you a more efficient running style.

Being light on your feet and minimizing contact time with the surface of the ground is also important. Although when running at a slower pace you will have more contact time, still concentrate on a feeling

of lightness as you cover the ground. Think of gliding across the surface rather than planting each foot down heavily.

You should also be aware of how your feet land on the surface – because when running they are going to be doing it lots of times.

Pronation is when your ankle rolls inwards after your foot has first made contact with the ground. Pronation is a normal part of the running gait and assists in the shock absorption process. Problems can occur when over-pronating (excessive pronation) which can lead to injuries in the knees, ankle joints or even in the back.

The opposite of pronating is supination, which is where the ankle rolls outwards. Again, supination is part of the gait cycle and the shock absorption process, but over-supination can also lead to injury. The easiest correction for both of these problems is to have the correct footwear.

Foot strike

1 Front-of-foot landing gives a good running form, but it has less shock absorption and will put a large amount of pressure on your calves.

2 Heel strike gives good shock absorption, but is often seen in slower runners and those who overstride.

3 Mid-foot runners enjoy a good balance of shock absorption and speed.

For most runners the best option with foot strike is to keep your natural style and allow your body to adapt as you run more. However, it is important to know which form you are adopting so you can adapt your stretching sessions accordingly. You will also need to change your foot strike if you are picking up re-occurring injuries.

The heel-coming-down-first style provides the best shock absorption, stretches out the calf muscles and will put less stress on your Achilles tendon. This style is quite body friendly but it is synonymous with slower running, poor backlift and overstriding. You will see a lot of straight-leg runners with a heavy heel strike.

Putting the front of your foot down first can help produce a more economical and faster running style. This is partly because you spend less time with your feet on the floor and it naturally leads to kicking your back heel up towards your backside. This style will also put less stress on your ankles and knees. Runners who use this style tend not to overstride and place their foot directly under their hips. The main problem with this approach is that the calf muscle is continually contracted and never gets stretched out. This is a major problem if you

are running for four or five hours and will contribute to shin splints, Achilles tendinitis and muscle pulls. Some runners who naturally put the front of their foot down first have also suffered with ITB problems. If you are a front-foot runner and you find it difficult to change then you should incorporate extra stretching sessions, with the main focus on the calf muscles and ITB. Along with regular sports massages, this can help prevent further injuries.

Mid-foot running, as you would expect, gives you some of the advantages

and disadvantages of the other two styles. So, you get a slight calf stretch with not to much pressure on the Achilles tendon and the ITB. However, you do get less absorption than on a heel-strike action. This can cause more problems in the longer races, simply because you are on your feet for longer and are putting more impact on your body for a longer period of time.

✓ Learn which part of the foot you are landing on first.

✗ Do not try to change your foot strike overnight.

✓ Incorporate the correct stretching for your particular running style.

✗ Don't ignore pains – it could lead to further injury.

✓ Have a light easy contact with the floor.

✗ Avoid a heavy heel strike and straight-legged running.

✓ Place your foot directly under your centre of gravity.

✗ Do not overstride.

Cadence

1 Concentrate on powering off your leg – this is what increases your speed.

2 Place your foot directly under your hips.

3 Concentrate on moving your energy forwards and not up and down.

Some aspects of technique are best left alone. This would be true of your running cadence (amount of strides per minute), but not with where your foot lands.

Your foot should land directly under your hips (your centre of gravity) as this prevents overstriding, which can cause injuries. This problem is normally associated with runners trying to run quicker. If you take longer stride lengths you will find yourself travelling faster. You will also find yourself picking up injuries such as sore knees, pulled glute and hamstring muscles, and the most common injury from regularly overstriding – shin splints.

If you watch most elite athletes the foot lands under the gravity of their body and the amount of strides they take – around 175 to 185 strides per minute (around 90 steps per leg) – is not too dissimilar to many recreational runners. So why are they going faster? The reason is because the power these runners use to push off from their legs is greater, so they will have less contact time with the floor. This means that per stride their body is travelling farther, even if the foot landing is in a similar position to a social runner.

You can do an experiment of counting your strides per minute in your warm up and then when you are running at a faster pace. Most people will find that they are using the same amount of foot strikes. As you progress through your training and you find yourself running faster this leg pace should remain the same. You will feel yourself getting stronger and pushing off your legs harder and thus covering more distance per stride.

Be aware that if you are getting muscle pulls in your glutes or the back of your legs then you are probably overstriding so make sure you are not placing the foot in front of your line of gravity. To get extra pace concentrate on pushing off your legs harder, kick your back heel towards your backside and have as little contact time with the ground as possible. You should imagine gliding across the surface and avoid bobbing up and down. You want your energy moving forwards, not up and down.

✓ Place your landing foot under your centre of gravity (your hips).

✗ Do not overstride.

✓ Keep your cadence at roughly the same pace.

✗ Do not increase the amount of strides in an attempt to go faster.

✓ To increase your pace kick your back heel up higher.

✗ Do not bob up and down.

✓ To increase pace have less contact time with the ground.

✗ Do not shuffle your feet.

Uphill

1 Pumping your arms on uphills gets the blood flowing and can help to clear lactic acid in your system.

2 Keep an easy relaxed running style and accept you will have to slow down on uphills.

3 Maintain your technique of placing your foot directly under your body and don't overstride in an effort to get the hill out of the way.

The biggest mistake you can make when running uphill is to tense up. Few people relish hills but they are a part of running. Relax your upper body, don't overstride, keep your arms moving forwards and backwards and concentrate on keeping your back heel kicking up. If you keep looking forward it will help you avoid tensing up, although some runners prefer to look down at the road so psychologically they can't see the hill ahead. Some runners also take smaller strides and pump their arms a little harder on uphills. This can get the blood flowing and help clear out the lactic acid.

Common errors on uphills are to lean forward and stride out further. This is often done in an attempt to speed up on the hills and get it over and done with. Keep your running form the same easy and relaxed style. The biggest adjustments you should make when running hills is your pacing and mental approach. Are you one of those people who dreads the thought of running up hills? By adjusting your pacing they will feel a lot easier.

The first thing to remember is that your body operates better if you keep it working at an even intensity level. You expend a lot of energy if you keep pushing the intensity up and down. To keep the intensity level you will need to run slower uphill. Your natural instinct will be to push hard to get to the top then ease off the intensity. Although you may be maintaining an even pace your intensity levels (heart-rate levels) are going higher on the uphills. A heart-rate monitor will enable you to check that your heart rate stays within five beats per minute of its level when you are running on the flat (although this does depend on the gradient and length of the hill).

Bear in mind an even approach is right for race day but not always for training, where you can push yourself up the hills. Working the hills hard will improve lactic thresholds, strength in your legs and your mental strength. You should also make certain that you run completely over the top of the hill and keep working yourself for another 50 metres.

A common error in hill training is to get to the peak exhausted and slow down. By keeping your pace even for that extra distance you will be giving yourself a more gradual lowering in intensity (which can prevent you feeling light headed). It will also give you extra mental strength so when it comes to race day you won't just ease off when you get to the top of a hard hill. This is the time you want to push a little harder in the race.

So the key to your hills is to keep your form even, keep your intensity levels even and learn to embrace the challenge. Hill running is excellent for increasing strength in your legs and mind and this will ultimately help you become a better runner on the flat as well.

✓ Keep your body relaxed.

✗ Don't overstride.

✓ Keep looking forward into the distance.

✗ Don't push too hard to get up the hill quicker.

✓ Embrace the challenge of taking on the hills.

✗ Don't fear hills – they are a part of running.

✓ Maintain your technique when running uphill.

✗ Don't lean forward into the hill.

Downhill

1 Try to increase your leg speed when running downhill.

2 Keep your body perpendicular to the hill.

3 Place your landing foot slightly behind the hip line.

When you are running downhill simply try to think of falling gracefully. Don't force it but instead allow your body to use the gravity to pick up pace as you head for the bottom of the hill and revel in the fact that you are conserving energy by using natural forces.

Running downhill can be very hard on your body, especially your back and knees, which can take a pounding. However, if you keep on fine-tuning your technique you will gain the confidence to really go for it. Then, gradually, you will find yourself running faster downhill, using less effort and not waking up in the morning with aching joints.

When running downhill concentrate on keeping your body perpendicular to the hill and avoid your natural inclination to lean backwards. Leaning back will cause more pressure on your lower back and you will consume more energy.

Keep your body propelling forward and ensure that you keep your posture tall and avoid shuffling your feet. The main difference between running downhill and on the flat is that you should place your foot slightly behind your hips. Instead of the normal technique of placing your foot directly under your hips it should land slightly behind your hip

line to reduce some of the impact, allowing you to fully utilize the momentum of the hill.

Many runners also increase their cadence (leg speed) on the downhill as this can lessen the impact on joints and increase pace at the same time. This is a technique to practise, as you may feel out of control on the descent when you first do this. At first you may feel like an elephant tumbling down the hill but over time you will feel as if you are skipping across the surface and benefiting from the momentum of the slope.

A lot of these techniques require a bit of faith and confidence in your ability. It is natural to put the brakes on when running downhill. Practise each technique a little at a time and you will slowly find yourself making up great time during the race overall.

When running downhill always be aware of the terrain you are running on. As you are running quite fast and pushing it hard so that you are almost out of control it will be hard to make sudden stops. Be aware of what is out in front of you, such as potholes, roads bisecting your route or any other obstacles which you may need to avoid.

If you have got your pacing up the hill correct then you will have some energy to really work a little harder when running downhill. Most runners, when they are starting out, will push too hard up the hills, then not work hard enough downhill.

✓ Think of falling gracefully when running downhill.

✗ Don't shuffle your feet.

✓ Increase your cadence.

✗ Don't slow down.

✓ Place your landing foot slightly behind the hip line.

✗ Be careful not to overstride.

✓ Keep your body perpendicular to the hill.

✗ Don't lean backwards.

fitness & training

// FASTER // FITTER // MORE MOTIVATED

Training zones

Training zones allow you to work at the correct intensity. When starting a training session it is important to know the reason you are training. What is your goal for this session and what do you want your mind and body to achieve? It is unrealistic to think that you can push your body 100 per cent every time you hit the water and the road. This is why training programmes start with a light workload and then have gradual increases. Even as the workload increases there will still be some lighter weeks that allow your body to recover.

A lot of your planning will depend on your training history. If you have prepared for an event before you will be more aware of what your body can sustain without suffering adverse affects. If this is the first time you are undertaking a more structured training programme, or if this is the first time you are training for a triathlon, you should try to follow the training programme you set out and take care not to get carried away (See Over-training and over-reaching on page 78).

There are also many positive aspects for working at the correct intensities. Improving different areas of training zones will enable you to get faster and stronger for longer periods, both mentally and physically. Working in the correct training zones allows you, even if you are training by yourself with little or no support, to prepare as the professionals do.

A lot of what we set out in this section is based around heart-rate monitors. If you are training without a heart-rate monitor, then you will need to use what we call Rate of Perceived Exertion (RPE). Imagine a scale of one to 10. One is little or no effort, while 10 would be your maximum effort. Where a heart-rate percentage is displayed, simply divide the figure by 10 to get the correct figure for yourself (eg 70-80 per cent of maximum heart rate would equate to 7-8 RPE).

Your heart-rate monitor will normally work out correct training intensities automatically for you. The equation below is included for those monitors that don't and also so you have some background information as to what the monitors are doing.

220 - your age - your resting heart rate. Intensity per cent + resting heart rate = target training zone

For example: an athlete who is aged 30 and has a resting heart rate of 70 beats per minute (bpm) training at 70 per cent of maximum heart rate will be calculated as follows:

220 - 30 - 70 = 120
70 per cent of 120 = 84 + 70 = 154 bpm

It is important to remember that you know your body better than your heart-rate monitor so if you are feeling very ill or dizzy and your heart rate is still low you may need to listen to your body, take down the intensity or even stop. You should also be aware that before aiming for your target training zones you should you be fully warmed up and allow time for your heart rate to climb to the training levels.

Endurance work
60-75 per cent of maximum heart rate

This intensity will normally make up the bulk of your work. You may also hear this referred to as the fat-burning zone, base training or train don't strain. With good technique and an injury-free body you should be able to sustain long periods of time in this training zone.

At this lower intensity level your body can cope with large volumes of time training. Your body should not be put under too much strain, allowing you to concentrate on perfecting technique. It is in this

zone that you will be putting in the long hours of hard work and this creates a really good base for your training as well as your body. Physically your body benefits from a stronger heart, the increased ability to take oxygen on board and using this oxygen more efficiently to help the body perform better. By constantly repeating the correct running action your muscles will soon remember what to do and in times of fatigue this can really help to sustain good technique, which will maximize speed and efficiency.

It is also in this training zone that your body will burn high levels of fat. By working at the lower intensity levels the main source of energy your body uses will be fat. Because you can sustain this lower level for longer periods of time and your main fuel is body fat, this equates to a lot of body-fat burning.

This is good news for most people and it can be very rewarding to see your body-fat percentage lower, as well as making you a better performer. After a sustained period of training sessions you will also notice that you can run farther while keeping your heart rate in the same training zone. For some people this happens remarkably fast and it can be really motivating to see the rewards so quickly.

Anaerobic/lactate thresholds
80-90 per cent of maximum heart rate

The above percentages really are just a guideline. The only way to truly establish your exact lactate thresholds is to be tested in a lab. Obviously many of us do not have this option as it can be expensive and requires taking blood.

Your next best option is to do a time trial of your own. Set a distance in your strongest discipline that is challenging to complete over a 20-30 minute period and then take your average heart rate over this period. If you feel halfway through the trial that you cannot continue due to muscle fatigue, or your muscles are 'burning', stop and see what your heart rate is as this can be a good indicator as to your lactate threshold.

What's happening and why does it matter? Without becoming too technical, when training at these levels of intensity, the main source of energy used is glycogen (which is stored in the muscles). A by-product of this is the release of lactate acid. Once this lactate acid accumulates to a certain level your performance will become greatly reduced. So by training at the correct levels it is possible to increase your thresholds and your body can then deal with

the release of the lactate acid more efficiently.

This type of training can greatly enhance your performance. Although it will be less in volume than the endurance work, training around these thresholds can give you the ability to cover longer distances at a faster pace with a lower heart rate. This lower heart rate means that you will produce less lactate acid and can continue with less muscle fatigue. You will be greatly surprised at the gains your body can make in these training levels.

Red-line zone
90-100 per cent of maximum heart rate

This zone is rarely used for endurance athletes. It is mainly used for speed and interval training and can only be sustained for short periods, even if you are very fit. Points to note are that the heart rate can be increased by other factors and may cause you to adjust your training zones accordingly. Dehydration, heat and altitude can all cause the heart rate to increase anywhere between seven to 10 per cent.

• *For more information on using training zones see pages 142-143.*

Over-training and over-reaching

The sensation of fatigue is necessary because it lets you know you are pushing your physical limits. You train to improve your performance and your body generally reacts positively to being 'pushed'. However, in certain circumstances, if your body is over-stimulated or stimulated incorrectly, you will suffer adverse effects.

Levels of fatigue

1. The first level of fatigue is hypoglycaemia – the term for abnormally low levels of blood glucose. You reach this when you have exhausted your glycogen stores, haven't ingested enough carbohydrates to produce more blood glucose and are still training or racing.
2. Post-training fatigue is the natural response to several hours of intense exercise, which tells you that you are pushing your normal training limits.
3. Over-reaching is the next step up and is when short-term performance drops and develops as a result of an intense training session. Symptoms are those of normal fatigue. The right amount of recovery will allow you to become faster and stronger. It is, however, a warning.
4. Over-training is the debilitating and long-term (often lasting weeks and sometimes months)

fatigue, which degrades rather than stimulates performance.

Over-training in volume and/or intensity can lead to some inevitable outcomes. Firstly, if you train too hard or over-train, your immune system will be very low, leaving you susceptible to illness. A cold can set you back a long way in your preparation. You would be amazed to what lengths top endurance athletes go to avoid illness.

The other potential problem you face is injury. Over-use of your muscles in training, where you are repeating the same action over and over again, can often lead to injury.

Burnout is another key issue to consider. If you keep pushing your body as hard as you can in every session for as long as you can you will eventually find yourself not wanting to train at all. Having a different target for each session will help you become mentally prepared every time you put on your training kit.

How to prevent over-training

The most frequent causes of over-training are: excessive increase in training loads, insufficient recovery periods, poor diet (insufficient quantity of carbohydrates or other nutritional elements), travel factors

and a lack of variety in your training.

So how do you prevent over-training? You need a balance between training and recovery in both the long term (mesocycle) and short term (microcycle). This means that after a few weeks of heavy training, the intensity should be reduced for a period of time (usually a week) and extra rest days can be introduced. The purpose of this recovery week is to allow your body complete regeneration.

Most training programmes include one or two rest days per week as well as a day or two of easy training, allowing you to recover. Unvaried training programmes without alternating periods of high and low volume/intensity also severely increase the risk of over-training. The key is planning your own personal training programme to occasionally over-reach but not over-train. Your challenge is finding your own individual boundary.

Building endurance

Swimming

The biggest mistake you can make during training is to view triathlon as three separate sports. If you swim, shower and go home with no thought of your bike ride then you set yourself up for problems later on, and the same goes for your cycling and running training.

The weekly long workout you do in each discipline will increase your aerobic capacity and build endurance over a period of time. As you come to the end of a long swim, for instance, pay close attention to your effort level and in particular your breathing. Avoid pushing too hard during these sessions and focus instead on keeping a steady pace you can sustain that doesn't lead to exhaustion.

Many swimmers favour the hard and fast approach, better suited to a 50-metre sprint than a triathlon, and end up exhausted. One good exercise for developing a smooth, leisurely style is to count the number of strokes you take to get from one end of the pool to the other. Over a period of time aim to reduce that number and notice how much more relaxed you feel.

By reducing your stroke rate and gliding farther after each hand entry you avoid wasting energy and are better able to regulate your effort levels over the course of the swim. Roll your shoulders and your hips with each hand entry and stretch out in front of you beneath the waterline as if you are being towed along.

Keep a record of the distance you swim at each long session and increase this gradually over the course of your training. Treat each increase as a test to see how you cope with pacing and finish with the all important question "Could I now cycle on these legs?"

Remember to ease back on the volume of training before a race. Reduce the long swim by as much as 50 per cent over the final two weeks and conserve energy. Don't make the classic mistake of attempting long, taxing workouts the day before a race, as this will undo months of training and undermine your performance on the day.

Rest is an integral part of any training programme, so make sure you build it into your schedule early on and learn to look after your body. Use your spare time to relax and unwind, and choose stress-free pursuits such as reading, listening to music and soaking in a hot bath.

Cycling

As the longest section of a triathlon is cycling, structure your programme accordingly and get used to being in the saddle for an appropriate amount of time. You may experience discomfort in the lower back and tightness in the hamstrings at first, especially on the longer rides, but this should diminish if you take it easy and only increase the distance gradually in your training.

Make sure you buy a bike that fits your physical dimensions (see cycling equipment on pages 18-22). One of the prime causes of discomfort and injury is having the wrong sized components that over-stretch muscles already tired from prolonged effort.

Make only slight adjustments to things like saddle height or crank length and assess the changes slowly over a period of time.

During long bike rides keep the same focus on pacing and try to maintain a smooth and consistent pedal stroke. Top cyclists often spin with an exceptionally high cadence, but attempting to achieve this in the early stages of your training may be counterproductive. Look for a happy medium, using gears that don't overtax your leg muscles and leave you with plenty to spare for the run.

Aerobars put you in a more aerody-namic position on the bike and technically make you faster, but be sure to get used to them in training first. Long periods spent hunched over in this position can stress your lower back and weaken your core muscles. Change your body position at regular intervals and relieve stiff muscles by stretching gently.

Certain elements can turn a long, leisurely ride into a grim endurance test. Things like headwinds, crosswinds, torrential rain and the seasonal vagaries of heat and cold can all make cycling extremely challenging. Make sure you prepare for extreme weather conditions at the outset and make the necessary changes to your kit in advance.

Much has been written about fluid intake during exercise and the need to avoid dehydration, particularly during longer workouts in hot conditions. Take water and sports drinks with you but avoid drinking excessively, which in extreme cases can lead to hyponatremia (water intoxication).

Hills can be a source of anxiety, especially during a race when fatigue levels are high and the run course is still to come. If your race includes hills it makes sense to train on them and to learn the techniques for conserving rather than squandering energy. For the heavier rider new to triathlon it pays to stay seated, as standing puts added pressure on the leg muscles and hastens fatigue.

Get used to fixing punctures! All cyclists dread the moment a tyre blows out, but during a race the experience can be particularly demoralizing. Keep a spare inner tube and a set of tyre levers with you and learn to change it as quickly and efficiently as possible.

Running

The training objective for each long run is the same for the bike: to build endurance and enhance the aerobic system. Remember that triathlon differs from other sports and requires you to start the run in a state of fatigue, having expended a good deal of energy in the previous two disciplines. For this reason alone pacing has to be the prime motivator.

Schedule your long run on days you feel rested and not after a punishing workout on the bike (unless you happen to be triathlon star Kevin Moats training for an Ironman Hawaii!) The purpose of endurance runs is to develop good pacing skills and build stamina, extending the distance gradually. Combined bike-and-run workouts are also integral to training but are best performed as a separate workout with adequate rest between.

Heart-rate monitors are excellent devices for telling you how hard you are working, but don't forget your own in-built system of awareness. The talk-test is a simple but effective way of gauging effort levels during exercise and requires you to repeat a short phrase at intervals. If you can say the phrase out loud without feeling breathless you have passed the test; if you are not able to you may need to adjust your pace accordingly.

Try to finish your long run in the same physical condition as you started. This has the dual purpose of honing pacing skills and building confidence and gives you a specific target to aim for. Building stamina in this way can take time so be patient and take it easy.

Train first for distance, then for speed later. This old training maxim applies to all endurance sports, but especially to triathlon with its added complexity of three disciplines in a single event. Speed is essentially a by-product, a quality influenced by genetics and enhanced by increased fitness levels, stamina and endurance.

Your running form will certainly influence the outcome of your longer workouts. To maintain an economical pace and offset the likelihood of injury shorten your stride length and increase turnover. This will help reduce impact stress and assist forward motion.

Fuelling is one of the most important aspects of endurance sport and needs to be given careful consideration. The body has enough stored glycogen to last for roughly two hours of exercise. Beyond this you need to supplement, preferably in the form of carbohydrates which are converted to energy.

Keep in mind the golden rule and never use anything during a race that you have not already tested in training. This applies to both food products and items of clothing, as any late changes can result in an unexpected, sometimes allergic reaction. Don't buy running shoes the day before a race, for instance, but leave a period of time so you are able to wear them in.

Mental strength

It is said success in sport is determined 90 per cent by fitness and skill (physiology, biomechanics, etc) and 10 per cent by mental strength. This 10 per cent is significant and can play a massive part in helping you to improve performance and extract more enjoyment from sport. It is an area that until quite recently was largely ignored by the sporting community but these days it is widely recognized as a key tool in every sportsperson's kit bag.

Developing your mental strength will help improve motivation and confidence, both during training (oh, those cold winter mornings!) and on race day. It will also help you perform better under pressure, including keeping any emotional distractions in check. You should ignore this part of your training programme at your peril; you could significantly compromise all your hard training if you haven't prepared mentally for an event.

Why only train your body when your mind needs training, too?

So how can 'mental strength' be measured? Obviously, this is difficult to do, and is quite subjective, but it is possible by answering a few key questions to work out your mental strength rating. Among these are (measure on a scale of one-five):

Mark one-five in the boxes below

☐ What is my current level of self-confidence?

☐ How much mental preparation do I commit to prior to an event?

☐ Do I always learn something, new or old, from my hard training sessions or races?

☐ Do I continually stretch targets for myself, both in training and racing?

☐ How good do I consider my levels of concentration to be, both during training and racing?

☐ How relaxed am I before an event?

☐ Do I forgive myself when things don't go quite according to plan?

☐ How well do I control negative thoughts?

☐ Do I feel I get the most enjoyment out of training and racing?

☐ How much do I enjoy the competitive element of racing?

Note any question where you recorded a score of three or less; these are the areas that perhaps need a little attention in terms of improving mental fitness. Most of these areas are covered later, with suggestions on how improvements could be made.

It is an undisputed fact that the workings of the mind and the body are linked – how you feel undoubtedly affects performance. Keeping the mind in tune with the body maximizes the possibility that improved performances can be achieved, and maintaining a positive mental attitude will soon bring results.

So how can we mentally prepare for training and racing? Much has been written about goal setting in sports and there is a very good reason for that: it works! The process of goal setting is designed to help increase confidence and motivation, which in turn will help improve performance. Most people are excellent at setting goals; sadly less of us are as good at achieving them. You have only got to look at New Year resolutions for that. So, why is this? Part of the reason is that many people have no focus to their goals but tend to choose things they feel they ought to do, rather than the things they want to do, or the things that motivate them. Also, they tend not to have any structure to their goals, which leads to a lack of focus and direction, and eventually they can peter out.

Many readers will be aware of the SMART approach to goal setting. SMART stands for Specific, Measureable, Achievable, Relevant and Time bound. This structure has been used for many years as a way of ensuring individual's goals are fit for purpose. However, SCCAMP can be expanded as follows:

- **Specific.** It is important that goals are specific and clearly understood. Any ambiguity could lead to a loss in focus.
- **Controllable.** Goals should be something within your control; anything which has strong external dependencies could lead to failure.
- **Challenging.** There seems little point in setting goals that can already be achieved. Stretching your targets are the requirement.
- **Achievable.** Again, there is little point in having a target that is always likely to be out of reach, such as running a marathon in under an hour. Unachievable goals are likely to demotivate.
- **Measureable.** If a goal is not measureable how will you know you have achieved it?
- **Personal.** The more meaning the goal has, the more you will be driven to achieve it (eg proving detractors wrong!). *"I was told when I was 18 that I was too small to be a good 800 m runner. I rather enjoyed proving them wrong there."* Seb (now Lord) Coe.

When developing goals, it is important to consider the type of goals that are likely to satisfy your overall objective of improving performance, namely outcome goals and performance goals. An example of an outcome goal could be "I want to finish in the top 50 of the next race I enter." Unfortunately you probably have no control over such a conclusion, as this could influenced by a whole host of external factors, and failing to achieve such a goal could lead to you becoming demotivated. It is better to set performance goals, where you do have control over the outcome, such as: "I want to be relaxed throughout, to keep focused, and to complete the race strongly."

It is essential you write these goals down and refer to them regularly. This will help provide a consistent link between what you are doing physically and what your ultimate aims are mentally. In addition, setting goals will set your subconscious to attract things that will support the goal.

The specificity of your goals can further be defined by the horizon you are choosing for your goals. A good tip is to maintain a multi-horizon set of objectives. For instance, choose two or three at 30 days ahead, a similar number at six months and perhaps a third set for 12 months. As each horizon approaches the detail for each goal becomes increasingly specific and a constant strategy for improvement is executed. Apply this across both training programmes and races.

Triathletes are renowned for their obsession with goal setting, driving on to improve PBs in each discipline. However, a study conducted a few years ago by the University of Kent, England, investigated whether perfectionism is directly related to performances in triathletes. The study identified two types of perfectionism: perfectionistic strivings, described as the desire to want to do better than others and improve one's own performance, and perfectionistic concerns, which is the opposite; a fear of doing worse than others and not improving on previous performances. The study concluded that only the former – perfectionistic strivings – had a significant positive effect on performances. So strive to outperform others, but at the same time do not worrying about underperforming, as this could have a negative effect on performance.

Two of the most important areas of mental fitness are motivation (being motivated, maintaining it, regaining it) and confidence, which is defined as 'a feeling of self-assurance arising from one's appreciation of one's own abilities or qualities'. These two areas contribute more to mental fitness than any other and it is by paying particular attention to these areas that significant performance improvements can be achieved.

But what is motivation? It is defined as 'a drive to fulfil a need'. Motivation drives us to do things; it is important because it energizes and directs our behaviour. Motivation is actually a personality trait and there are two main types – motive to avoid failure (in other words avoid tasks which could be measured as failure by others) and a motive to achieve success. An example of motivation in a sporting context would be a penalty shoot-out in football. Some players are motivated to achieve the success of scoring a penalty, others are motivated by the fact they really don't want to miss (fail).

Of course, there comes a time when everyone's motivation starts to wane a little and it is important to recognize that this is likely to happen to you, particularly during long training sessions between competitive races. So what can you do? Try a few of these ideas:
- Keep an eye on your sleep levels. Increasing the amount of sleep can improve performance and assist recovery. Physical training takes its toll on body and mind and both need to properly recover.

- Cross training helps relieve boredom and burnout. Rest days and light training days also help maintain a healthy mental state.
- Listening to music relaxes and empowers. Or perhaps try watching sport recordings for inspiration and technique.
- Consider meditation which will certainly help focus and concentration.
- Revisit your purpose. If you ask "Why?" enough you will be able to return to your inner values.

Triathlon is an endurance sport and maintaining high levels of concentration and motivation during both training and racing may, in some cases, be counterproductive. If this is the case for you, developing dissociation strategies for the longer legs of events can help to remove the constant worry of whether you are going to make it though the event. Just focus on the 'mechanical' aspects of that particular discipline (eg count the number of strokes in your head, or try and concentrate on cadence during the cycle leg, and so on).

Maintaining a positive mental attitude also helps to maintain healthy motivation levels, particularly during a tough training session or race. Thoughts in your head will influence you, so it is surely better to keep more positive thoughts

in the head than negative ones? The conscious mind has difficulty processing negation. If you are asked not to think of the colour blue, you have to think of the colour blue to process the information.

The use of imagery techniques will help maintain a positive approach, particularly for a race event. Try the following:
- Imagine yourself at an event, just before the start, feeling relaxed and positive and confident.
- Use all your senses to obtain a full all-round 'image' of the day. Imagery is sometimes referred to as 'visualization', but this infers the use of a single sense so a better term is imagery, which allows the use of all the senses. 'See' the other competitors lining up, 'hear' the hubbub of the watching crowd, 'feel' the breeze on your face etc.
- Imagine yourself starting the race, swimming strongly and confidently, passing other runners, feeling happy and in control.
- If you are aware of any steep hills on the course, imagine yourself pushing up these, enjoying the burn as you move smoothly along. This is quite important. The conscious mind can sometimes blur an imagined event with a real event, so if you have already 'cycled' up the steep hill, you know what to expect because you have

experienced it already, at least in your mind. This is called a 'future memory'.

- Now, imagine the final stretch, running strongly and confidently up to the finish line, in an excellent time. Give yourself another 'future memory' of someone handing you a well-deserved cold drink (or whatever your usual 'reward' is) at the end of the race!
- Try to run through this imagery a few times before the race. In this way you can be quite prepared for the race itself.
- Some people include minor problems in the imagery race so as to prepare themselves for all eventualities. Perhaps a change in the weather, or a dog on the course, or whatever. This way they will have already 'experienced' the event, and can prepare themselves accordingly.

It is also a good idea to keep a diary of your training, focusing on those sessions you feel most excited about. Referring to these regularly, particularly just before you go to sleep when your mind is most susceptible to suggestion, will instil a sense of positivity and will also help you to maintain high levels of motivation.

So, we arrive at race day. What kind of things can we exploit to ensure we maximize all that hard physical training so we really enjoy ourselves on the day? Here are a few ideas for you to try:

- Have a last look at your diary, remind yourself of the excellent training sessions or races you've enjoyed, get yourself feeling relaxed, confident and positive.
- Replay the imagery of the race in your mind again, 'remember' how excellent your race is going to be.
- Don't try to 'eat the elephant', particularly for longer races. This means break up the race into manageable chunks and focus on each chunk as you approach it. For example, for the run focus only on the first kilometre, keeping the pace steady, with relaxed breathing. Then focus on the next kilometre, and so on. This can be a powerful tool.
- Use triggers to maintain focus. As we are aware, it is easy to lose concentration during a race, so choose a couple of key words or phrases such as "Push on" or perhaps "Stay relaxed/strong/ controlled", and when you repeat them in the race itself they can help trigger the necessary focus.
- If you approach a steep hill during the run leg try looking straight down to the ground. By doing this, any gradient is removed from sight (and therefore mind) and covering the ground will look the same as running on the flat so running

becomes easier. Of course, you should be sure that no obstacles are coming up and that you have a clear run. Safety should be your priority here.
- Don't beat yourself up about things that don't go to plan. Recognize this has happened, plan to learn from it and move on. Certainly don't let the negativity fester. Remove it and return to a positive mind-set. It is vital to focus on what you can control during a race. If you concern yourself too much with the things that are outside of your influence you will be wasting unnecessary energy and potentially lose focus on the things you can influence.

After the race it is always a good idea to conduct a 'three and three review'. Focus on three things that went well and three that didn't go as planned. In this way you can remain positive and take strength from the things that were successful, while not allowing yourself to become complacent but at the same time give yourself something to learn from.

After you have spent a little time developing your mental fitness, return to the questionnaire at the beginning. You should see improvements in a number of areas, which means you are developing an edge to your triathlon skills that your fellow competitors may lack!

cross training

// STRONGER // TOUGHER // MORE POWERFUL

The basics

You might think that you already have enough on your plate simply training for a triathlon. After all, intensive sessions of swimming, cycling and running will surely get you fit enough.

So why cross train then?

Here we focus on four reasons to cross train: strengthening a weakness in a particular muscle or muscle group, injury prevention, motivation and ensuring that you maintain your general fitness.

Most coaches will include a strength-training programme into an athlete's schedule whatever sport they are involved in. The amount of work that needs to be done in the gym can vary from sport to sport and, of course, the distance you are training for and the specific goals you have.

Generally, the shorter events will require more power and strength, which can be gained with weights. If you are entering a longer event it is advisable that the strength training is done well away from your heavy training sessions in the pool or on the road. For example, if you are considering entering an event in six months, start your gym work with heavy weights and low reps (eight to 12 reps) for six to eight weeks, then

lower the weights but increase the reps (maximum 15) for a couple of weeks. After this you can then start to cut back on weight work.

However, everything depends on how serious and challenging your targets are. You can keep working on the strength training after these guidelines but be aware that your other training could be affected if you suffer from muscle fatigue. If you don't want to give up your cross training completely you could substitute gym work for increased core work or specific stretching exercises. Overall, then, the benefits of spending time in the gym will be extra power, but don't overdo it – your training should always keep your core goals in mind.

Identify and strengthen weaknesses in the chain

One benefit of cross training is targeting a particular weakness in your body that is holding you back in triathlon. Once you have identified that weakness in your body while training or through analysis from a physio you can head to the gym and really focus on that particular area, whether it's your legs or simply building up muscle groups for general body balance. So, for example, if you find some weakness in your hamstrings (back of the leg) and glutes (backside)

while running you can use squats (see page 100 and 102) and bench steps (see page 104) to strengthen these areas. By focussing on these muscles in the gym you really will notice a difference.

However, it must still be remembered at all times that a lot of the pain we experience is due to the build up of lactic acid and the best way to combat this is to train in your chosen sport to keep the essential muscles in active use. You will get stronger from your swim, cycle and run training, as muscle adaptations occur.

Injury prevention

Prevention of injury is probably the main reason to do specific training for your sport. Injuries can ruin months of hard work and for us non-professional sportspeople, as well as ruining the sporting dream, this can make daily life very uncomfortable – just ask anyone with bad back pain they picked up in sport who has to sit in an office for eight hours a day.

For example, if your hamstrings become very strong and tight and your opposite muscles (the quads) are weak then this can cause the pelvis to be held in a tilted alignment, which in turn causes poor back alignment and back pain. For these reasons, in the workout

Legs – lunges

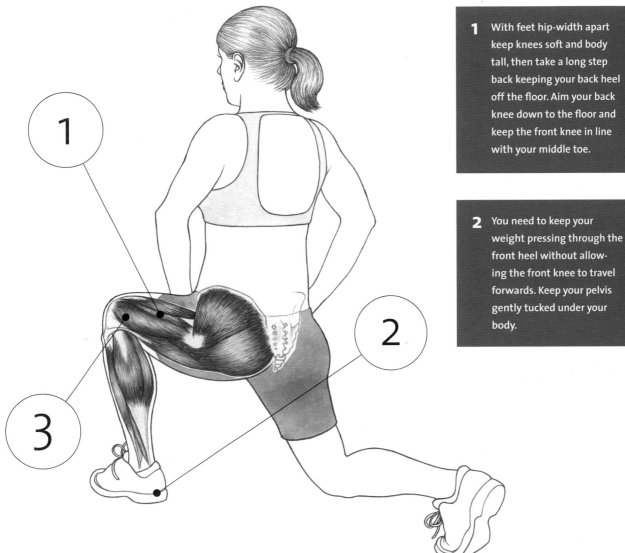

1 With feet hip-width apart keep knees soft and body tall, then take a long step back keeping your back heel off the floor. Aim your back knee down to the floor and keep the front knee in line with your middle toe.

2 You need to keep your weight pressing through the front heel without allowing the front knee to travel forwards. Keep your pelvis gently tucked under your body.

3 The feel of the lunge movement is straight down and up. There should be no forward movement. This will keep the pressure on the front knee.

Muscles used

Primary: quads, glutes, hamstrings, calves.

How will it improve my triathlon?

Cycling: increased leg strength increases aerobic capacity and time-to-exhaustion. Ride faster with more power and less fatigue.

Legs – single leg squats

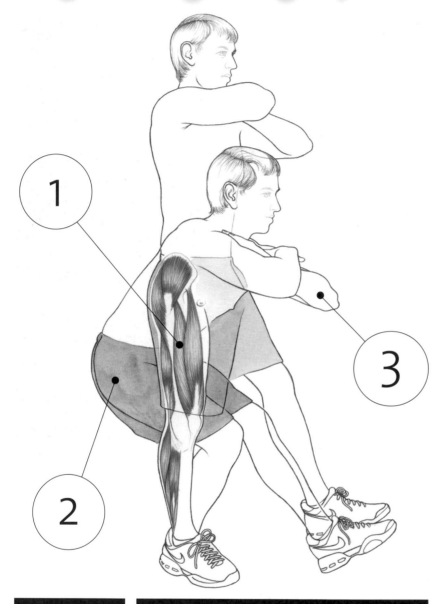

1 Standing on one leg, have the other leg bent at a right angle with the knee at hip height. This is the position you will start and finish each rep.

2 Keeping the posture tall throughout the rep, bend your supporting knee and sit back as if you are about to sit on to a chair.

3 This exercise is as much about balance as strength. So when starting you may want to use a wall as support. Lose this support as soon as possible to gain all the benefits.

Muscles used	How will it improve my triathlon?
Primary: glutes, quads, hamstrings, calves. Secondary: lower back.	Running: this gives extra strength and stability of one leg, which is how we run. All the muscles of the legs you use to run will be working. This can also help create a better alignment when you run, so preventing pronation and supination.

Legs – single leg hops

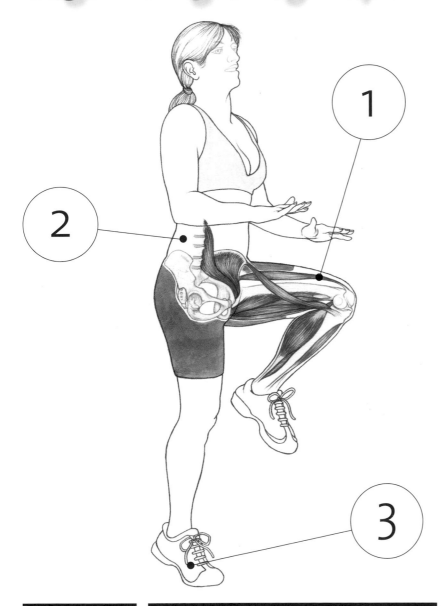

1 Just like the single leg squats, start standing on one leg and have the other leg bent at a right angle with the knee at hip height.

2 Hop as high as you can, making sure that you do not bend forward or lean back. You should try to land on the same spot that you took off from.

3 To prevent any damage to your back or knees the landing in this exercise is crucial. Make sure you are cushioning your landings as if you are landing on a mattress.

Muscles used	How will it improve my triathlon?
Primary: glutes, quads, hamstrings, calves.	Running: this is a great exercise to give you power when you push off your leg, control when landing on your leg and all the stability you will need when running.

Legs – bench steps

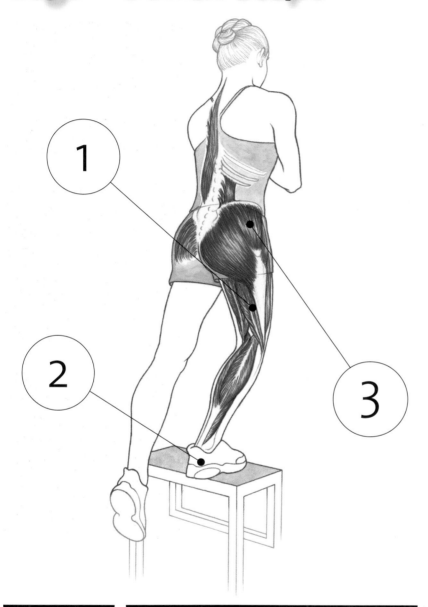

1 Stand about 30cm (about 12in) away from a step or bench. Step one foot up before bringing the other leg up, always keeping the foot and knee at a right angle.

2 When stepping onto the bench with your first leg, carefully put the heel down first. This will keep your body secure on the bench and activate the correct muscles.

3 Always keep the body straight and tall. The temptation is to lean forward from the hips. To increase the intensity you can hold a weight in each hand.

Muscles used	How will it improve my triathlon?
Primary: quads, glutes. Secondary: hamstrings, calves.	Cycling: strong leg muscles and muscular endurance help prevent fatigue and this freshness will help you to maintain sharp reflexes and your technique.

Legs – lunges with one foot on ball

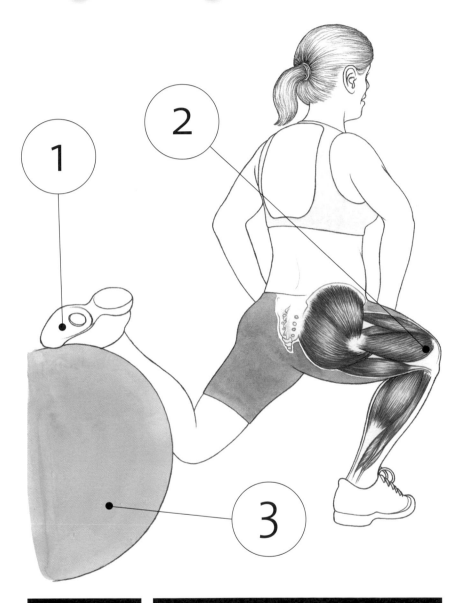

1 Have the top of one foot on the ball behind you. The weight should be on your front foot, which you should position as far forward as possible.

2 Bending the front leg make sure that your knee goes no farther forward than your ankle. It should lower down to a 90-degree angle. Think of going straight up and down with all your weight pressing through the front heel.

3 This is an advanced exercise and requires strength and co-ordination. If you need the wall for support use it until you can manage without. If you don't have a exercise ball, you can use a more stable base such as a bench.

Muscles used

Primary: quads, glutes, hamstrings, calves.

How will it improve my triathlon?

Running: this exercise will strengthen all the running muscles of the leg. It will force you to use one leg so you become equally strong in balance on both sides. Remember you use both legs to run.

Back – dead lift

1 Start with your heels under your hips, legs slightly bent, your back straight, hands just wider than your thighs and palms facing the body. Then lower the bar down to your knees by leaning forwards and concentrating on working your back. Pause briefly and come back to your starting point.

2 As you go through the reps keep your back long and do not allow any flexion or extension from your knees. Shoulders should be pulled back at all times.

3 All the weight should be in the heel of your foot and your knees soft without bending them. Avoid doing squats.

Muscles used	How will it improve my triathlon?
Primary: lower back, hamstrings, glutes.	Swimming: this is an important drill to maintain strength in your lower back and backside.

Shoulders – bent-over rowing

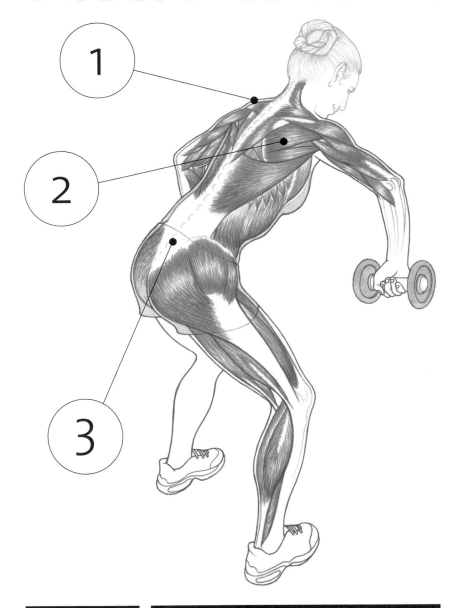

1 Start with the weights down by your knees. Stay in this bent-over position and squeeze the weights in towards the belly button in a rowing movement, before straightening your arms to the starting position again.

2 When lifting the weights feel your shoulder blades squeezing together. This will concentrate the workload in the centre of your back.

3 Staying in this position can be tough on your lower back and there is a temptation to curve your lower spine outwards. Avoid this by keeping your pelvis in the correct alignment and squeezing your abs.

Muscles used

Primary: neck, shoulder and back (trapezius). Secondary: biceps.

How will it improve my triathlon?

Cycling: strong shoulder muscles help you to stabilize the handlebars when pedalling hard, especially while pushing hard and climbing steep hills.

* To do this exercise without weights, start in the same position but put both feet on a resistance band and pull round in an arc from your shoulders in the same path to the top as with weights.

Chest – lateral pull down

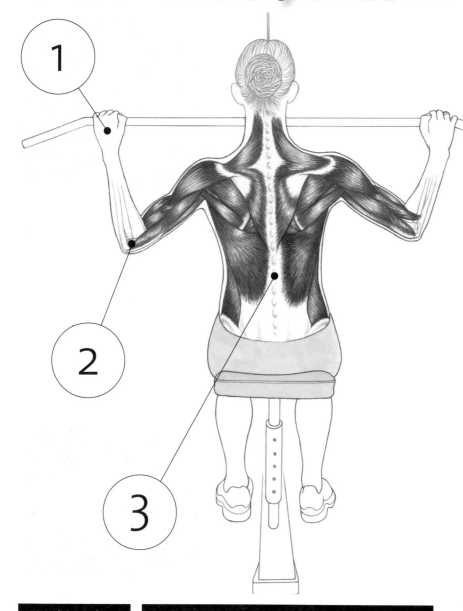

1 Hands should be positioned one and a half times of your shoulder width apart. Keep your body tall and lean back slightly. Pull the bar down towards the upper chest and keep control and then release back to the starting position.

2 Feel your elbows as you pull down as this will activate your back muscles. Keep your hands light on the bar – if you grip too hard your forearms will fatigue quickly.

3 As your body fatigues avoid allowing your back to swing and your backside to come off the seat. Also avoid pulling down quickly.

Muscles used

Primary: laterals.
Secondary: biceps.

How will it improve my triathlon?

Swimming: an important muscles group for freestyle. The more power you can generate from here, the more water you can move to propel yourself forward.

Chest – press-ups

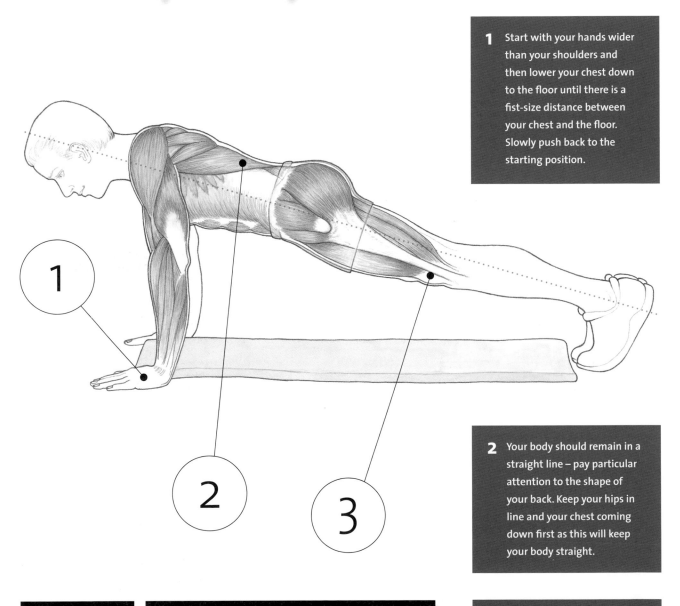

1 Start with your hands wider than your shoulders and then lower your chest down to the floor until there is a fist-size distance between your chest and the floor. Slowly push back to the starting position.

2 Your body should remain in a straight line – pay particular attention to the shape of your back. Keep your hips in line and your chest coming down first as this will keep your body straight.

3 You can lower your knees down to reduce the intensity of the press-up. You should also do this if you feel you are losing your body alignment.

Muscles used

Primary: pecs.
Secondary: triceps.

How will it improve my triathlon?

Running: this exercise will help keep your posture tall, promoting that ideal running stance. It will also keep your body in good overall balance.

Arms – bicep curls

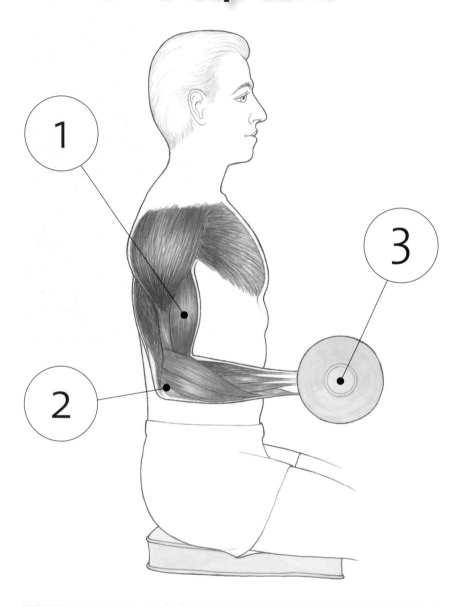

1 Hold the weights with your palms facing forwards while keeping your hands at a natural carrying grip. Bend at the elbow and curl the weights to your chest. Pause briefly then curl back to the horizontal starting position.

2 Keep your elbows close to your body and do not allow them to pull back behind the body alignment.

3 Your hands need to remain strong but soft. If you grip too hard you will feel your forearms work more as opposed to your biceps.

Muscles used	How will it improve my triathlon?
Primary: biceps.	Swimming: you are not trying to look like Charles Atlas so don't overdo this one – look for tone not size. This exercise helps you to improve power in the upper arm, which is important through your stroke.

* To do this exercise without weights, start in the same position but put both feet on a resistance band and pull round in an arc from your shoulders in the same path to the top as with weights.

Arms – tricep dips

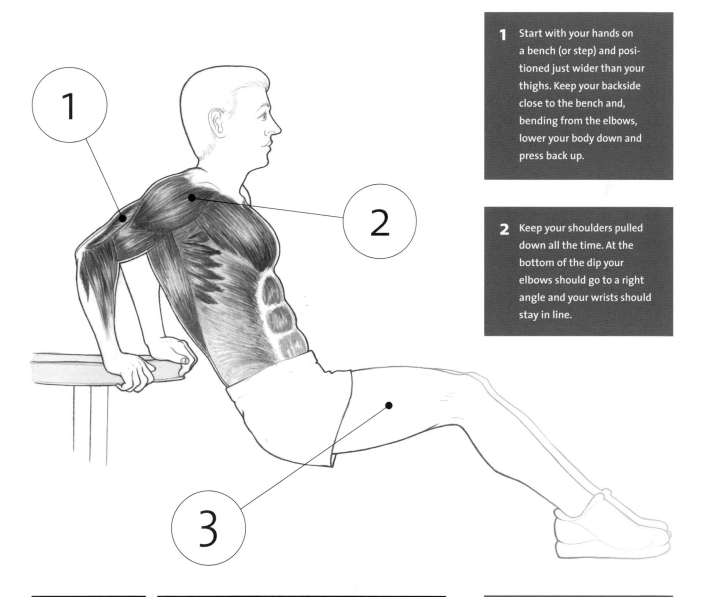

1 Start with your hands on a bench (or step) and positioned just wider than your thighs. Keep your backside close to the bench and, bending from the elbows, lower your body down and press back up.

2 Keep your shoulders pulled down all the time. At the bottom of the dip your elbows should go to a right angle and your wrists should stay in line.

3 You can make this exercise more intense by straightening your legs and flexing your feet. When doing this keep your backside close to the bench.

Muscles used	How will it improve my triathlon?
Primary: triceps.	Swimming: triceps play a major role in the pull stroke in breaststroke and by toning them up you will make yourself more efficient. This also works some of the chest muscles to maintain tone.

Core – hip abductor

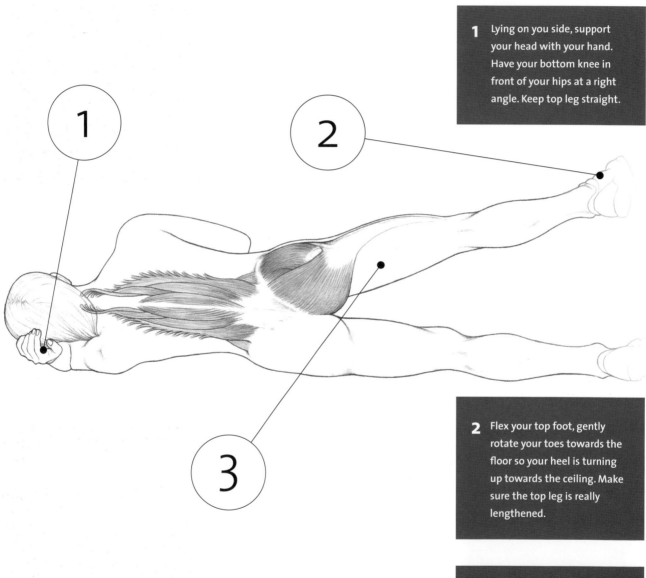

1 Lying on you side, support your head with your hand. Have your bottom knee in front of your hips at a right angle. Keep top leg straight.

2 Flex your top foot, gently rotate your toes towards the floor so your heel is turning up towards the ceiling. Make sure the top leg is really lengthened.

3 Gently pulse the top leg up and down 10 times. Then create small circles one way 10 times and reverse and repeat the circle 10 times. Repeat this set two to three times.

Muscles used	How will it improve my triathlon?
Primary: glutes	Running: this exercise really isolates the glute med. This muscle is used in stabilizing the hips, which helps in the prevention of runners' knee.

Core – front plank

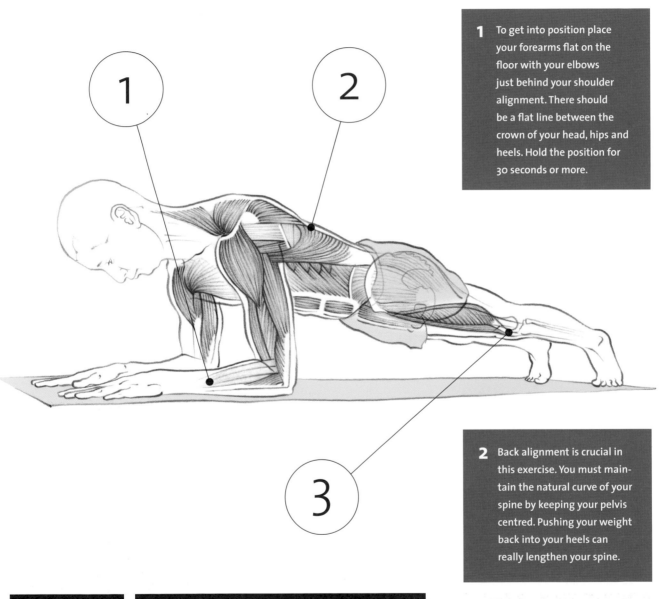

1 To get into position place your forearms flat on the floor with your elbows just behind your shoulder alignment. There should be a flat line between the crown of your head, hips and heels. Hold the position for 30 seconds or more.

2 Back alignment is crucial in this exercise. You must maintain the natural curve of your spine by keeping your pelvis centred. Pushing your weight back into your heels can really lengthen your spine.

Muscles used

Primary: deep and superficial abs and lower back.

How will it improve my triathlon?

Cycling: your torso is an integral part of the pedal stroke. A strong torso provides the rigidity to deliver maximum power from your quads to the pedals.

3 If you cannot maintain the correct alignment, gently lower your knees to the floor. You should do this for a lower intensity option.

Core – side plank

1 To get into position place one hand on the floor with your elbow in a direct line under your shoulder. Your hips should be stacked one on top of the other. Then lift up as if you are drawing away from a flame until your body is in position as per the illustration. Hold for 30 seconds or more.

2 As with the front plank the key is body alignment. Your back must maintain its natural curve – lengthen your legs as this will help to keep your back long.

3 A lower intensity alternative of this exercise is to bend your knees at a right angle so your feet are behind and lift up on your arm while balancing on your knees. This can be used if your shoulders are weak.

Muscles used

Primary: side abs, deep and superficial abs and lower back.

How will it improve my triathlon?

Swimming, cycling and running: this exercise works on your arms and maintains core strength, which is important in preventing back injuries. Ensure you do it left and right-handed to keep your muscles balanced!

Core – leg raises

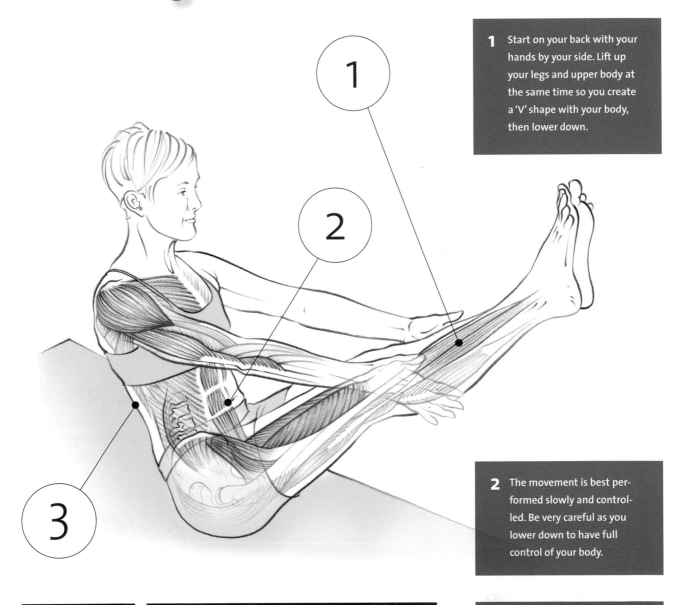

1 Start on your back with your hands by your side. Lift up your legs and upper body at the same time so you create a 'V' shape with your body, then lower down.

2 The movement is best performed slowly and controlled. Be very careful as you lower down to have full control of your body.

3 This is a tough exercise and performed incorrectly can cause injury to the back. A good option to start with is to keep the knees bent as you come up.

Muscles Used	How will it improve my triathlon?
Primary: top of leg and abs, hip flexors.	Swimming, cycling and running: mainly one for your abdominal muscles, giving similar benefits to sit-ups and maintaining core body strength. Helps develop leg strength and suppleness in your lower back.

Core – back raises

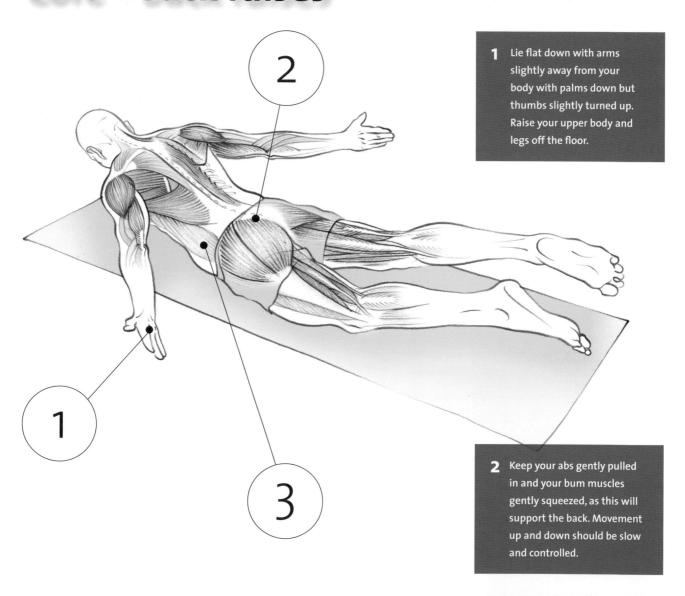

1 Lie flat down with arms slightly away from your body with palms down but thumbs slightly turned up. Raise your upper body and legs off the floor.

2 Keep your abs gently pulled in and your bum muscles gently squeezed, as this will support the back. Movement up and down should be slow and controlled.

3 If you want more support for your back place your hands under your shoulders for support and push up from the floor. Use as much or as little pressure on the hands as you need.

Muscles used

Primary: lower back.

How will it improve my triathlon?

Cycling: this exercise is great for cyclists because it helps to strengthen your lower back muscles and hamstrings, which are especially important during climbing.

Workout programme – beginners

Sets x2, reps x8-12 (core raises, back raises x15 reps), 1 min recovery between exercises.
Planks: aim for 30 second holds (reduce if losing technique).

To find your ideal weight for each exercise you should be able to complete the reps but just about hit failure on the final rep. As a guide, the heaviest weight you would use would be for your larger muscle groups (eg glutes and quads used in squats) and the lightest weight you would use would be for your smaller muscle groups (eg biceps in bicep curls).

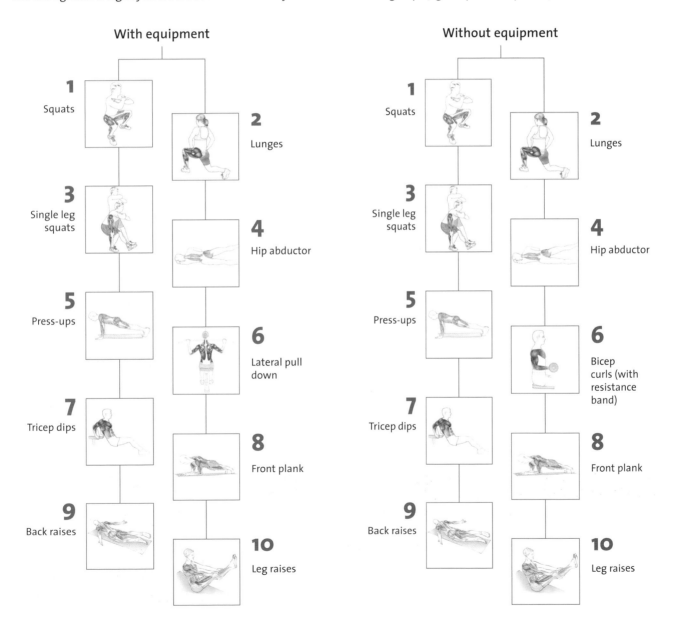

With equipment

1. Squats
2. Lunges
3. Single leg squats
4. Hip abductor
5. Press-ups
6. Lateral pull down
7. Tricep dips
8. Front plank
9. Back raises
10. Leg raises

Without equipment

1. Squats
2. Lunges
3. Single leg squats
4. Hip abductor
5. Press-ups
6. Bicep curls (with resistance band)
7. Tricep dips
8. Front plank
9. Back raises
10. Leg raises

Workout programme – intermediate

Sets x2, reps x10-15 (core raises x20 reps)

Planks: aim for 45 second holds (reduce if losing technique)

To find your ideal weight for each exercise you should be able to complete the reps but just about hit failure on the final rep. As a guide, the heaviest weight you would use would be for your larger muscle groups (eg glutes and quads used in squats) and the lightest weight you would use would be for your smaller muscle groups (eg shoulders in bent-over rowing).

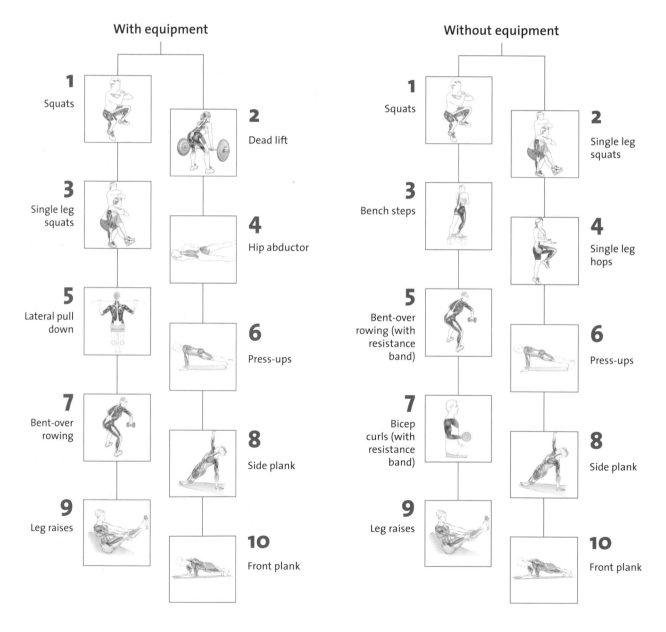

With equipment

1 Squats

2 Dead lift

3 Single leg squats

4 Hip abductor

5 Lateral pull down

6 Press-ups

7 Bent-over rowing

8 Side plank

9 Leg raises

10 Front plank

Without equipment

1 Squats

2 Single leg squats

3 Bench steps

4 Single leg hops

5 Bent-over rowing (with resistance band)

6 Press-ups

7 Bicep curls (with resistance band)

8 Side plank

9 Leg raises

10 Front plank

Workout programme – advanced

Sets x3, reps x12-15 (core raises x30 reps)

Planks: aim for 1 min to 1 min and 30 seconds holds (reduce if losing technique)

To find your ideal weight for each exercise you should be able to complete the reps but just about hit failure on the final rep. As a guide, the heaviest weight you would use would be for your larger muscle groups (eg glutes and quads used in squats) and the lightest weight you would use would be for your smaller muscle groups (eg shoulders in bent-over rowing).

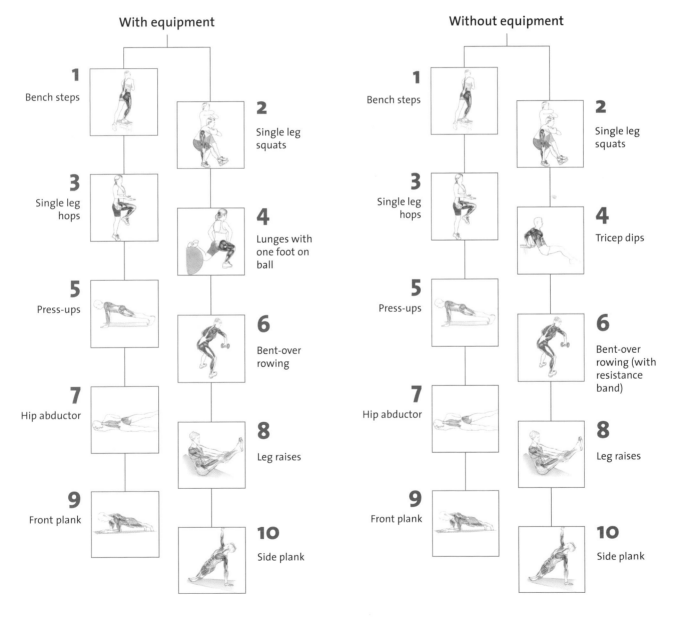

With equipment

1 Bench steps

2 Single leg squats

3 Single leg hops

4 Lunges with one foot on ball

5 Press-ups

6 Bent-over rowing

7 Hip abductor

8 Leg raises

9 Front plank

10 Side plank

Without equipment

1 Bench steps

2 Single leg squats

3 Single leg hops

4 Tricep dips

5 Press-ups

6 Bent-over rowing (with resistance band)

7 Hip abductor

8 Leg raises

9 Front plank

10 Side plank

nutrition

// HEALTHIER // LIVELIER
// MORE ENERGETIC

The basics

Food and nutrition are the basic elements for a correct training regime in any sport. Think of your body as if it were a car – it could have the most powerful engine, the most aerodynamic shape or the best design but it would never run without its fuel. Food is the natural fuel for your body.

Food can be divided into four basic groups: **carbohydrates, proteins, fat** and **liquids** and each one of them is equally important in running our body, giving it energy, stamina, resistance and self-recovery. Each one of these elements is essential to our nutrition and is absolutely harmless to our health and body if taken in the right amounts, balanced in combination with all the others.

Carbohydrates are the fuel for your muscles. They provide the energy for your muscles to work.

Proteins build and repair muscles whenever they have been stressed during exercise.

Fats are energy stores for your body and help the correct functioning of the cells and maintaining your body's temperature.

Liquids maintain the right body fluid concentration and expel toxins.

A correct combination of each one of the above-mentioned elements, adjusted depending on the sport and your body's response, will provide you with the correct nutrition needed, both for training and competition.

A basic diet for an athlete or an active person (someone who trains three times a week for more that 60 minutes per training session) should amount to a daily intake of 3,000–4,500 calories per day, according to the sport and the amount of training. This might seem a lot more than what you heard in your sports club or while chatting while jogging but remember that this diet is not planned in order to make you lose weight but to give you an understanding of what your body needs to perform at its best while under the athletic stress.

If you eat the right foods at the right time, plan your weekly diet with the same care you use to plan your training, weight will never be a problem and you will understand how a correct diet (as a plan to correctly feed your body, instead of a rush into weight loss) will drastically improve your life as well as your athletic performance

Nutrition in sports is as important as the exercise. Again, your body,

as a car, needs the right fuel to perform at its best.

There are four key steps you need to understand before planning your diet:

1. Do not get too hungry as it will make you take the wrong dietary choices and swallow whatever you can find. Have at least five meals a day, calibrating the amounts at each meal.
2. Eat at least three different kinds of foods at each meal as mono-eating will make your body incapable of digesting correctly what you don't usually eat. Choosing different kinds of vegetables, fish and meat, will provide your body with different vitamins and minerals.
3. Always balance the food elements at each meal. Every meal should be based on carbohydrates combined with proteins and fats (amounts change from person to person; but a good starting base is a balance of 50 per cent carbohydrates, 30 per cent proteins and 20 per cent fats).
4. Try to choose foods in their natural state. A banana is better than an energy bar and an orange is better than orange juice for instance.

Assess your diet

People tend to be obsessed by their body shape. It is a normal feeling given the kind of images the media world sends us every day. When you assess your ideal diet, try to forget about your shape and think realistically for a moment about what goals you want to achieve athletically. By doing so you will be more focused on understanding, planning and applying the correct diet to everyday life.

First question: do you have breakfast?

Eat breakfast every morning. If you train early in the morning try to wake up half-an-hour before you normally would just to make sure you eat a good amount of food for breakfast. If waking up earlier is going to be impossible, try to eat more carbohydrates the night before, and top up the next morning with some snack. It's very important for you to eat something one hour before training, as it will guarantee the sugars flow in your blood, while the muscles will use the energy stored during the night.

Avoid hyper-protein breakfasts. Remember that every meal should be based around carbohydrates. A little sample of ideal food for breakfast would be:

- Porridge with cottage cheese or ricotta cheese and some nuts.
- A cup of milk or yoghurt over a bowl of cereals with a banana and some raisins. Remember that all-bran cereals tend to be stressful for the bowels, which is inappropriate for training and competition. Also avoid sugar-coated cereals.
- A sandwich made with two slices of whole-grain bread and 60 grams of smoked salmon (you could add a some light cream cheese) and an orange or a glass of orange juice.
- Muesli with yoghurt and one piece of fruit.

If you feel the need for a boost of caffeine, feel free to drink it, as it would not interfere with your training (although it gives stomach acidity to some people). No person is the same, which means it's up to you to find your right intake by calibrating and testing day after day to find the right proportions and taste to suit you.

Second question: do you snack after training?

Remember that eating and drinking after training is the only way you can start to refuel your empty muscles. You can choose what kind of snack you should have, depending on the amount of energy spent and the length of the interval before your next training session. This is the moment where you really train your muscles to intake and store more and more glycogen.

You have two options: either you go for a low or a high GI snack. GI is the acronym for Glycemic Index which is a measure of the effects of carbohydrates on blood sugar levels. Carbohydrates can be released into the blood slowly (in that case they have a low GI) or quickly (high GI). Although important for the control of illnesses like diabetes, the control of the GI is something that most athletes don't really worry about. What you must decide is the kind of recovery you want from your diet.

If you have two training sessions in one day, or another training session the morning after, then you might want to consider a high GI recovery, choosing food like corn flakes, white bread, watermelon or baked potatoes. On the other hand, it's been shown that a low or medium GI recovery, because of its slower release of sugars, will be more effective in the long run, using food like fruits, vegetables, whole-grain breads, pasta, milk and yoghurt.

Remember that gulping down gallons of protein shakes after training will be almost useless.

You need mainly carbohydrates to refuel your muscles and only some proteins to recover the stressed muscles and help them rebuild.

Third question: do you ever go hungry during the day?

If you do sometimes go hungry in the day you need adjust your plans to make sure this doesn't happen. Make sure you plan your meals and snacks beforehand by experimenting with your meals for a few days and organize your day around the food you know you will need.

Ideally you should have one substantial breakfast before leaving your house, one snack no longer than four hours after breakfast (between 10.00 and 11.00 for most people), one lunch (if you think it would be better then prepare it the night before, in order to avoid rushing into eating any food you find in the shops when hungry). Then have another snack three to four hours later, a good dinner (try to avoid pasta, rice and bread for dinner, unless preparing for a competition or the night before the competition itself) and one last evening snack.

Fourth question: do you find yourself fatigued during training?

There could be different reasons for being fatigued during training.

- A low glycogen storage. The glycogen has been burned and you are now using your proteins and fats as fuel, provoking your blood to carry ketones to your brain. In this case you should eat more carbohydrates before training and more carbohydrates after training, in order to teach your muscles to store as much glycogen as possible.
- Dehydration. A lack of liquids means your body can't cool down properly, endangering the health of you cells and making the expulsion of carbon dioxide and lactic acid more difficult.

Carbohydrates

One of the many myths you may have read is that carbohydrates are fattening. This is untrue. Fats are fattening, carbohydrates are the basic fuel you need to eat in order to have enough energy in your muscles. In a sports diet carbohydrates are an absolute must of your nutrition requirements.

Carbohydrates can be divided into two groups: simple and complex. Simple carbohydrates are monosaccharides (single-sugar molecules: fructose, glucose and galactose) and disaccharides (double-sugar molecules: table sugar, milk sugar, honey and refined syrups). Fruits and vegetables contain many different kinds of carbohydrates, which is one of the reasons why your diet should include a good variety of vegetables and fruits.

During digestion your stomach turns the sugars and carbohydrates into glucose, before the latter is then turned into a polymer (a chain of five or more sugar molecules) called glycogen. Glycogen is the key to your energy levels. Glycogen gets stored in your muscles and your liver, supplying your body with the right amount of energy for your training or your competition.

While the glycogen stored in your muscles will function as an energy reserve to move your body and train your muscles, the one stored in your liver will provide a slow-release of sugars into your bloodstream, guaranteeing a constant amount of sugars to your brain. This is important, because the sugars in your brain will influence your performance drastically.

Did you ever hear about, or ever hit the infamous 'wall'? The wall is something many professional athletes have hit during their career. It's a moment during which you become sure you are not going to make it to the finish. The wall is not a metaphysical concept, it is simply the moment when you have no more sugars flowing to your brain. Having the right amount of glycogen stored in both your muscles and your liver will help you avoid the wall.

What is the main difference between the different sugars, then? While refined sugars, soft drinks and energy drinks will only provide an energy supply, vegetables and fruits will supply, along with different amounts of glucose, also vitamins and minerals which will help spark and run your body engine in the correct way.

Always try to eat foods in their natural state. Whole-wheat breads, brown rice, brown pasta, as all the nutritional elements you will find in unrefined products, are more valuable than the ones you will find in refined ones. The same concept can be applied to cooked carbohydrates – it is preferable to undercook vegetables, in order for them to retain the vitamins and minerals contained in them along with the sugars and starches. This leads to a very important point you should be aware of. Your muscles need to be trained not only through exercise, but also by making them capable of storing the biggest amount of glycogen possible. How do you do that? By eating the right carbohydrates in the right amount.

During training you put your muscles under stress in order to grow them and make them stronger. At the same time, by supplying them with the right amount of carbohydrates, you will teach them to store more glycogen.

In 100 grams of untrained muscle you can store only 13 grams of glycogen but the same amount of trained muscle will store about 32 grams, while a muscle trained to be loaded with carbohydrates will be able to store between 35 and 40 grams. Needless to say, the latter is the muscle that will perform better and for longer.

1 Unrefined food will have a better nutritional value than the refined ones. Wild rice, whole-wheat breads, brown pasta, popcorn (unbuttered), oats and porridge, raw fruits and vegetables, etc.

2 Always make sure that any meal you take during the day is based around carbohydrates. Try to think in terms of the proportions stated above (50-30-20).

3 Vary your food as much as possible. A good way is to plan your meals by colour (green leaves or broccoli, tomatoes, peppers, carrots, oranges, apples, blueberries, etc).

4 Always make sure that before and after training you have the right amount of carbohydrates to restore your energy levels and sugars in your bloodstream. Once the glycogen is used up your body will start burning your fat as an energy supplement. Although this is the basic concept of how to trim down your stomach, bear in mind that such a process is detrimental to your performance, as your bloodstream will carry ketons to your brain instead of sugars, amplifying your tiredness and affecting your mood.

Proteins

Let's start by refuting another myth: proteins do not make you stronger, exercise does. There is always a magic aura around words such as proteins and amino acids, believed to be the mysterious ingredients to a muscular body. Don't worry, it's not so mysterious.

Proteins have many different roles in your body. They help build new muscles, repair those stressed by exercise, are the reason your hair and nails grow, energize your immune system and, above all, help replace red blood cells. A protein-based diet is useless. Drinking protein shakes, eating too many egg whites, or stuffing yourself with chicken breast will lead to poor results. An over-intake of proteins can even be counterproductive. Your body can store only a certain amount of protein or amino acids and if you exceed this they will be either burned for energy (a scarce amount if compared to carbohydrates) when the body runs out, or stored as glycogen or fat. There are two main problems you can face if following a diet with too much protein.

1. It will prevent you from eating the right amount of carbohydrates, lowering the amount of energy stored in your muscles.
2. It will break down into urea, an organic compound your body eliminates through urine. People who eat too many proteins will need to increase their fluid intake to eliminate as much urea as possible, leading to frequent visits to the toilet.

By eating too many proteins you also increase the chance of eating excessive fats (through meats, and condiments) that your body will store. The correct amount of protein an athlete can digest varies but as a rule of thumb, is calculated to be between 1.2 and 1.6 grams per body weight kilogram per day. That is usually less than your daily intake by only eating meat, fish, dairy products or legumes. The ideal intake would be a daily total of about 150g to 200g, adding the proteins you should get from two servings of low-fat dairy products (milk, yoghurt and cheese) per day.

Meats can be divided in three kinds: white meats, red meats and fish. An ideal sports diet should include all kinds of meats in your weekly plan.
- Fish is the best option as the fats it contains are unsaturated (including the famous Omega-3), so is a better choice than the saturated fats commonly found in meats and dairy products.
- White meat is preferable to red meat as it usually contains less fat (if it is either breast or properly skinned thigh and drumsticks).
- Lean red meat, although not the healthiest option, should be eaten between three and four times per week. Red meat contains iron and zinc and iron is an essential part of haemoglobin, a protein that transports oxygen to your muscles and brain. If you are missing the right amount of iron you could suffer fatigue and exhaustion. Zinc is a mineral that plays a big role in removing carbon dioxide from your muscles when you are exercising. A good red meat is venison as it contains a lower quantity of saturated fat.

With dairy products, you should eat low-fat. Semi-skimmed milk and yoghurt are close to the ideal intake percentage (they contain a percentage of 40 per cent carbohydrates, 35 per cent proteins, 25 per cent fat), so are a perfect snack. It's an easy way to eat proteins and also supply vitamin D and calcium and the right amount of potassium, phosphorus and riboflavin. Potassium and phosphorus help your body in metabolizing the calcium to strengthen your bones, while riboflavin is a vitamin that helps your body to transform the food into energy.

1 Choose fish before white meat or red meat, but make sure you eat all three kinds during the week.

2 Include proteins in every meal.

3 You can find all the proteins you need in the food you eat – you don't need to use shakes, bars or pills.

4 Try to eat low-fat dairy products at least once, preferably twice a day.

5 Do not overfeed yourself with proteins, as it is useless.

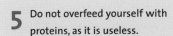

Fats

Fat is as important in your diet as any other food element. Fat helps provide the temperature regulation of your body, helps the health of skin and hair and provides a safety coating for your internal organs.

The most important thing is to know what kinds of fat you should eat and in what quantities. Fats can be divided into hard fats and soft fats. Hard fats are the fats that come in the form of meat lard, chicken skin or butter, while soft fats, the ones you should favour in your diet, are in the form of olive oil and canola oil.

As mentioned earlier, calories from fat should correspond to about 20 per cent of your diet. The most important thing to remember is to stay away from Hydrogenated Trans Fats, which are a very unhealthy result of a chemical process that adds hydrogen to both mono and polyunsaturated fats.

Don't be afraid of eating fats during your resting periods. Many people think if you don't exercise your muscles will turn into fat and you will gain weight. That is untrue. Muscles and fat are two distinct components of your body and you will only gain weight by taking more calories from fat than the ones you are burning, which, in the doses that have been mentioned before, is very unlikely.

You might have seen people in the gym torturing their abs, hoping to lose their belly by over-exercising the part closest to it. What you need to understand is that you lose your excessive fat by exercising the whole body and consuming the calories that you have taken. Let's put it this way: if you want to lose fat, you need to grow your muscles (in the whole body), as bigger muscles consume more calories. Don't try to over-stress specific areas of your body, as this is useless.

Remember that fats are what gives taste to your food, helping to make it more favourable to your palate. As you are making an effort to stick to a dietary plan for your athletic training, try to enjoy it as much as possible, adding the right amount of healthy fats to your meals.

1 Olive oil is a monounsaturated fat and is the best choice. Always try to buy extra-virgin olive oil and use it to cook and dress any food you want. The ideal amount should be around two teaspoons for each meal.

2 Nuts – like walnuts, almonds, pistachios, macadamia, Brazilian nuts, pine kernels, olives – are also a good choice for fat intake. Each one of them is a different size and contains a different amount of fat, so it's important to weigh them so you know approximately how many you need. For example: cashew nuts, peanuts, almonds, pine kernels, require a dose of nine grams per meal while walnuts, macadamias, hazelnuts, pecans and pistachios are about seven to eight grams per meal. For avocado and green olives allow a bit more (about 18 grams for the avocado and 30 grams for the olives).

3 Fish oil is another good choice, as it is rich in healthy fats. However, not many people like the taste and it would be a pity to waste a whole meal because of it.

Liquids

Water is the base of life. Your body is made in the most part by liquids and any loss of liquids has to be quickly restored.

Water does the following.
- It keeps your blood liquid, helping the correct transportation of oxygen, glucose and fat, while taking away carbon dioxide and lactic acid.
- It helps keep your body cool by absorbing heat from your muscles, sweating the heat out, cooling the skin through evaporating sweat and allowing the cooled down epidermis to cool the blood that cools down the organs. It's a positive vicious cycle.

Thirst is the most common sensation our body delivers to make us aware that we need to restore our balance. This sensation becomes more complicated when we deal with sports however.

There are many variables to be taken into consideration when you are exercising. There is the level of preparation, the weather, the fact your mind is focused on a goal, your body is too well trained or, because of the water on your body, you don't feel the heat. Bear in mind that, while exercising, your brain will communicate 'thirst' to you when you have already lost about one per cent of liquids and then it might be too late to rehydrate yourself. At that point your heart is beating more than needed, burning more glycogen than it should. At a two per cent loss you are officially dehydrated and at three per cent your body could be impaired in continuing the task.

The secret is to plan your drinking as well as your eating. Evaluate the amount of liquids you lose during a training session. To do so, weigh yourself naked before the training and right after, before drinking. The difference in weight will tell you the amount of liquids you lost. Your urine should always be a pale yellow; if it is dark and dense it means that there are too many metabolic wastes compared to the amount of water.

It takes between eight and 12 hours before your body becomes fully rehydrated so always plan your drinking during both your everyday life and training. By sweating you not only lose liquids but also electrolytes such as magnesium, potassium, sodium and calcium.

Always start your training session fully rehydrated from the session before by drinking between five and eight millilitres per kilo of your body weight. You can add sodium to your drink or chose a sodium enhanced drink, as it might help retain the water in your body.

You can use sodium in food and beverages after your training if you need to rehydrate quickly for a second session (up to 12 hours after the first one). Drinking between 30 per cent and 50 per cent more fluids than the ones you lost during exercise should be enough to re-establish the right concentration of liquids in your body.

Try to stay away from alcohol as much as possible. It causes strong dehydration as it is a potent diuretic and it would make you waste more liquids than you should. Also remember alcohol is a depressant and it suppresses drastically your motor skills along with your mood.

Pre- and post-competition planning

Before the competition

Your pre-competition training should be winding down (tapering) in the few days before the event (see page 142). This is because your muscles need time to recover from hard exercise. During this time, while you are reducing your training load you should be re-establishing the glycogen in your muscles, rehydrating yourself and mending the stressed muscles by eating some proteins.

Try to interpret your pre-competition training as a final rehearsal for the real event. Some people think that stuffing themselves with pasta the night before the competition will be enough but things are a bit more complicated than that.

During training you will have taught your muscles to store a good amount of glycogen in order to have a good reserve in every training session. The more you train your muscles with exercise, the more glycogen your muscles will be able to store, if educated to receive it.

From one or two weeks before your competition you should slowly increase the amount of carbohydrates by about 100 grams per day. The day before the competition itself you should start loading your body with carbohydrates from breakfast time.

Every athlete reacts differently to a competition. Some have no problem having a good dinner the night before – others find it difficult to digest food because of the excitement or worry. Therefore, start loading yourself with carbohydrates from breakfast.

And, if you feel like eating dinner try to vary the type of carbohydrates as much as you can. Pasta by itself might do the trick, but remember that fruits and vegetables contain slow sugar-releasing carbohydrates and they will help for endurance the day after. Avoid bran flakes or anything that you know could lead to stomach problems.

Every sport has its pros and cons when it comes to taking on liquid. Cyclists will crow that they can always carry their liquids with them and never need to waste time, while for swimmers, once the event has started, that's it for liquid intake. Runners are somewhere in-between these two examples. In well-organized races it is rarely necessary to carry any liquid as these will be provided at regular refreshment stations along the way. However, it is always worth checking beforehand just how frequent these stops are and what type of liquid is on offer. Rather carry a bottle of drink than go short on your regular intake of liquid (or your preferred drink) during a run.

Training brings a different dimension and you may be happy to carry what you need for your run. There are alternatives to being a pack horse, however, such as planning your route via places you know have water taps or shops where you can buy a drink (don't get caught up worrying about the few seconds it takes to buy a drink). Another alternative is to drive the route before your run and drop your drinks at regular intervals en route behind bushes or walls and then simply stop and pick them up on your run.

On the morning of the competition, according to the time the event starts, there are few rules you need to follow.

- Make sure you wake up in the morning with the right fluid balance. You can easily determine it by the colour of your urine.

- Start by having a big glass of water and breakfast or, if the competition is too early to have breakfast, make sure you load some more carbohydrates one hour before the event. This

will make sure that your liver will produce enough sugar to be delivered to your brain throughout the duration of the competition.

• Drink your water between one to two hours before the race so you can expel it before the race starts.

After the competition

As you will have seen, after the event you need to let your body recover by rebalancing the glycogen and the fluids. Take advantage of the first hour after the event, as it will be the period when you body will assimilate all the nutrients best.

Carbohydrates mixed with a little protein is the best option to have both glycogen delivered to your muscles while reducing the emission of cortisol, the hormone that breaks down your muscles during exercise.

According to whether you will have a short or a long time before the next competition, you will have to find the right way to fully recover your muscles and blood.

Different athletes prefer different solutions according to their experience. The main thing is to plan a good nutrition schedule. If you know you have to compete in a number of competitions that are close together, you might want to plan your diet starting from the week before, in such way that it will be faster to recover between the events.

If you have two events back to back you want to make sure you will recover immediately after the first one by over-loading yourself with high-GI carbohydrates and liquids that will restore not only the fluids but also the electrolytes (some sport drinks do that). Try to drink

as much as possible and judge the level of rehydration from the colour of your urine and comparing your weight before and after the event. If you happen to have more than two competitions in a span of more than two days, keep in mind that slow-GI carbohydrates have been proven to be more effective in the long run.

If you have enough time to recover after the event (one week), make sure you rebalance your fluids and have a little snack combining carbo-hydrates and proteins in the usual balance and then take your time, by simply starting the nutritional plan where you left it before the prepa-ration to the competition.

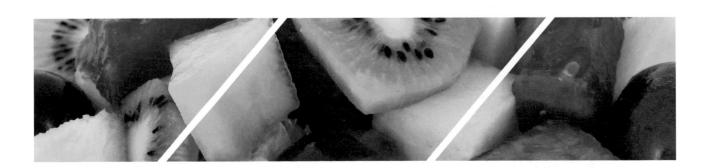

training programmes

// PLANNING // PREPARING // READY TO RACE

The basics

In an ideal world we would all have one-on-one coaching, access to laboratory testing to measure our fitness levels, and unlimited time in which to train. Instead, most of us have to fit in workouts around busy schedules and seek improvements in less specialized ways.

The training programmes in this book will help you plan towards your goal event, whether that be a sprint distance or an Ironman. Whichever programme you choose, read the appropriate guidelines first and make sure your current fitness is suited to that particular workload before you start.

Primarily, there are four elements that influence the outcome of any training programme.

- Technique
- Volume
- Intensity
- Rest

Technique (See pages 26-71) applies throughout to all the disciplines and, if practiced diligently, can improve both speed and economy and lead to major performance breakthroughs at all levels.

Volume is the total amount of weekly training and can be increased or decreased according to the time of year and the purpose of the training period.

Intensity refers to the level of effort you put into each workout and getting it right has a huge bearing on fitness, often meaning the difference between you reaching peak performance and burnout during races.

Lastly, and most importantly, rest has to figure into the equation to maximize the benefits gained from training and minimise the risk of injury. Rest is important; always factor enough rest into your training programmes.

Devising your own personal plan

The best results come from a programme that is designed specifically for you, the individual. Progress depends on a number of variables, including age, weight, current health, time constraints and motivation. The more of these factors you take into account, the better able you are to design a plan that works for you.

Use the training programmes at the back of this book as a guide and be prepared to change the format to suit your schedule, rather than the other way round. If you can't fit a session in because of work commitments, for instance, reschedule it or cancel it altogether. The same goes for the length of the workout. If you find the stated set too long or too taxing for your current ability, reduce it to something more manageable and make similar adjustments to the rest of the programme.

The opposite may be true for someone coming to triathlon from, say, a strong running background. In this case, the volume of run workouts may need to be increased to allow for this factor. But whatever your previous experience, keep in mind the three-sports-in-one principle and integrate them all into your personal plan.

Many triathletes fall into the numbers trap and become obsessed with the distance clocked up in training. Avoid making this common error and look for gradual improvements based on quality workouts, rather than those that appear to merely fill in time. If you have to miss one or more workouts for whatever reason, don't feel you have to make up the deficit later in the same week but simply resume the schedule when next possible.

Training plan and training zones

The maxim 'fail to plan, plan to fail' applies to every event you might enter, from a charity 5 km run to an Ironman. Triathlon is a complex sport in terms of both execution and equipment and requires organization to prevent confusion. By planning your training schedule well in advance, you isolate problem areas like nutrition and transitions and gain confidence week by week.

The training plan is divided into three phases (Base, Build, Peak) each lasting a set number of weeks, and each with a different focus. Fitness is built incrementally and in stages, resulting in peak performance at the time of the goal race. To reduce the risk of over-training and to maximize fitness, a taper period is introduced two to four weeks before the race.

Base phase
This early training period focuses primarily on building the aerobic system with extended workouts performed at a fairly low intensity. Experienced triathletes can include some speed work during the base phase, but this is not advisable for beginners. If you are new to the sport and/or have not exercised much in the last 12 months, use this period to slowly extend the length of workouts but keep the intensity to a minimum. One long workout in each discipline increases gradually week by week to build stamina and aerobic capacity in direct proportion to the distance of the race. Concentrate on skills and technique in all three disciplines, with special attention paid to any areas of weakness. Experienced triathletes often incorporate over-distance training for shorter distance races with the highest volume done during this phase.

Build phase
Workouts now adopt a more 'race-like' feel. Experienced triathletes schedule in brick workouts (training in two disciplines in the same workout) with intervals at, or near, race pace to increase muscular endurance and approximate the demands of the race. Beginners are best served by continuing to increase distance rather than intensity and learning to pace themselves accordingly.

The long weekly workout in each discipline continues to increase, peaking two to four weeks before the race. Swim-to-bike and bike-to-run workouts are performed as dress rehearsals, with a transition area set up as per race day.

Peak phase
This is the phase when fitness levels and endurance skills gained from previous weeks are at a premium. For more experienced triathletes workouts include race-pace bricks with extended intervals at higher intensities. Recovery needs to be a priority during this phase, as the risk of injury and burnout is far higher.

The weekly programme is structured around one, or possibly two, key workouts that emulate a particular aspect of the race. Where appropriate, bricks can be performed with short intervals at faster than race pace to recruit speed endurance muscle fibres and enhance stamina. Long workouts with intervals at high intensity need to followed by a suitable period of rest and recovery.

Taper
The length of taper depends on certain factors, including current level of fitness, volume of training and race length. Those training with high weekly volumes, or for long distance races, are best served by a taper of up to four weeks. This also applies to experienced triathletes with a high level of fitness who will benefit greatly from cutting back over a longer period.

Volume is significantly reduced during the taper period but frequency of workouts is maintained to prevent loss of form. Beginners can continue to increase the distance workouts closer to the race date, provided they continue to respond favourably.

(Active) rest week

Each training block has a built-in rest week that allows mind and body to adapt to the workload. The effect is achieved by a reduction in volume rather than frequency and cuts overall training time considerably. For beginners, every third week is a rest week. For all other programmes, every fourth week is a rest week.

The Training Zones

Aside from technique, you now know that volume, intensity and rest are critical to improvement. Gradual increases in distance at low intensities enhance the aerobic system and utilize your body's fat-burning capabilities, helping you train longer. Adequate rest allows the body to absorb these workouts and for the muscles to adapt and grow stronger.

Intensity is the key player, yet is perhaps the least understood and most often abused of all the elements in the training programme. A common error is to train at the same pace all the time. This leads to a plateau in fitness levels and prevents recruitment of muscle fibres better suited to the demands of a race. The other error is training either too hard or too easy for the workout in question. This has a similar negative effect and prevents the body from adapting sufficiently to progressive training loads.

To understand intensity it is necessary to have some knowledge of heart-rate percentages and ideally to use a heart-rate monitor (See pages 74-77). Most triathlon training is spent in Zones 1 and 2 to build a strong aerobic system.

Zone 1 (50-60% max heart rate)

Low-intensity workouts conducted at an easy to moderate pace. Zone 1 stimulates recovery from harder workouts by removing toxins from muscles and ensuring nutrients are replenished. It is the ideal intensity for long-distance workouts during the base phase, where pacing is a priority. Beginners training should be mostly in Zone 1 as it puts less stress on the system and needs less recovery time.

Zone 2 (60-70% max heart rate)

Training at a higher intensity recruits more of the endurance muscle fibres. Slow-twitch muscle fibres are capable of sustaining longer workouts at easy to moderate effort levels performed below the aerobic threshold. Training at lower intensities also helps the body metabolize fat for fuel and preserves finite stores of carbohydrate for harder efforts later on.

Zone 3 (70-80% max heart rate)

Key physiological changes take place at this intensity, including recruitment of speed endurance muscle fibres and a greater propensity for your body to burn carbohydrate. Significant time spent above the aerobic threshold reduces your ability to sustain distance and hastens fatigue. Experienced athletes sometimes use this zone during base training to prepare for higher intensity workouts in the next phase.

Zone 4 (80-90% max heart rate)

Zone 4 training utilizes muscle fibres equipped for endurance and speed, but once the anaerobic threshold is reached the duration of exercise is limited. As this zone is associated with higher levels of fatigue and muscular stress, don't spend long periods training here. Beginners are better avoiding this zone altogether until one to two years base training has been established.

Zone 5 (90-100% max heart rate)

This zone is suited to those engaged in short, fast activities and relies on a different exercising system less commonly used in training for triathlon. At the highest intensities, fast-twitch muscle fibres are recruited that burn carbohydrate as the primary fuel. Training at this zone can produce speed benefits similar to Zone 4, but the recovery cost is significantly higher and is only be appropriate for advanced triathletes.

• *For more on training zones see pages 74-77.*

Key to using these programmes

Swim training includes repeats with rest intervals. For example, 4x100 +10, 3x200 +20, Zone 1-2, means swim 100 metres four times with a 10-second rest between each set, followed by three 200-metre swims with 20 seconds of rest between each set. The intensity should be at Zone 1-2 (see page 143). Where you see RP (eg 1x200 RP) this means the set should be completed at race pace. Where you see alt (eg 12x50 alt) this means do one interval hard followed by one interval easy.

Brick training (eg Cycle/Run) means you are expected to train in two disciplines on the same workout. For example, Cycle/Run, 30 min/10 min, Zone 1 means cycle for 30 minutes and then run for 10 minutes at Zone 1 intensity (see page 143).

Transition run (eg Cycle/T-run) is intended to get your muscles used to the change in disciplines. For example, Cycle/T-run, 90 min/5 min, Zone 1 means cycle for 90 minutes, then a short five-minute run, all at Zone 1 intensity (see page 143).

Sprint distance: unfit beginner

		MON	TUES	WED	THURS	FRI	SAT	SUN	TOTAL TIME
BASE 1	Wk 1	Swim 4x50 +60 Zone 1	Cycle 20 min Zone 1	Rest	Run 15 min Zone 1	Swim 4x50 +60 Zone 1	Rest	Cycle/T-run 30 min/5 min Zone 1	1 hr 40 min
	Wk 2	Swim 4x50 +60 Zone 1	Cycle 20 min Zone 1	Rest	Run 20 min Zone 1	Swim 4x50 +60 Zone 1	Rest	Cycle/T-run 40 min/5 min Zone 1	2 hr
	Wk 3	Swim 2x50 +60 Zone 1	Cycle 20 min Zone 1	Rest	Run 15 min Zone 1	Swim 2x50 +60 Zone 1	Rest	Cycle/T-run 30 min/5 min Zone 1	1 hr 40 min
BASE 2	Wk 4	Swim 6x50 +60 Zone 1	Cycle 30 min Zone 1	Rest	Run 20 min Zone 1	Swim 2x100 +60 Zone 1	Rest	Cycle/T-run 40 min/10 min Zone 1	2 hr 20 min
	Wk 5	Swim 8x50 +60 Zone 1	Cycle 30 min Zone 1	Rest	Run 25 min Zone 1	Swim 2x100 +30 Zone 1	Rest	Cycle/T-run 50 min/10 min Zone 1	2 hr 40 min
	Wk 6	Swim 4x50 +30 Zone 1	Cycle 20 min Zone 1	Rest	Run 20 min Zone 1	Swim 4x50 +60 Zone 1	Rest	Cycle/T-run 40 min/5 min Zone 1	2 hr
BASE 3	Wk 7	Swim 2x100 +60 Zone 1-2	Cycle 40 min Zone 2	Rest	Run 25 min Zone 1	Swim 3x100 +60 Zone 1	Rest	Cycle/T-run 50 min/10 min Zone 1	3 hr
	Wk 8	Swim 3x100 +60 Zone 1-2	Cycle 40 min Zone 2	Rest	Run 30 min Zone 1	Swim 1x200 +60 Zone 1	Rest	Cycle/T-run 60 min/10 min Zone 1	3 hr 20 min
	Wk 9	Swim 2x100 +30 Zone 1	Cycle 30 min Zone 2	Rest	Run 25 min Zone 1	Swim 2x100 +60 Zone 1	Rest	Cycle/T-run 50 min/5 min Zone 1	2 hr 30
	Wk 10	Swim 4x100 +30 Zone 1-2	Cycle 40 min Zone 2	Rest	Run 30 min Zone 1	Swim 2x100 +30 Zone 1	Rest	Cycle/T-run 70 min/10 min Zone 1	3 hr 40 min
PEAK	Wk 11	Swim 2x200 +60 Zone 1-2	Cycle 40 min Zone 2	Rest	Run 25 min Zone 1	Swim 1x400 +60 Zone 1	Rest	Cycle/T-run 40 min/5 min Zone 1	2 hr 30 min
RACE	Wk 12	Swim 2x200 +60 Zone 1	Cycle 30 min Zone 1	Rest	Run 20 min Zone 1	Rest	Cycle/Run 15 min/5 min Zone 1-2	RACE!	1 hr 30 min + race

Transition training, the so-called fourth discipline, can be done on a day of easy training. Lay out your equipment as you would on race day and practise the mechanics of the transition. You may also wish to do this during brick training.

Note: it is sometimes difficult to stay in Zone 1 for the duration of a workout as a number of elements (eg hills, fatigue etc) tend to push your heart rate up. In these instances, aim to bring your effort back down as soon as possible.

Pre-race workout: the workout on the day before the race should be performed at a low effort level but with short bursts at a higher intensity to stimulate muscles in readiness for the race.

Sprint distance: fit beginner

		MON	TUES	WED	THURS	FRI	SAT	SUN	TOTAL TIME
BASE 1	Wk 1	Swim 4x50 +60 Zone 1	Run 10 min Zone 1	Cycle 30 min Zone 1	Swim 2x100 +60 Zone 1	Run 15 min Zone 1	Rest	Cycle/T-run 30 min/5 min Zone 1	2 hr
	Wk 2	Swim 6x50 +60 Zone 1	Run 15 min Zone 1	Cycle 30 min Zone 1	Swim 2x100 +30 Zone 1	Run 15 min Zone 1	Rest	Cycle/T-run 45 min/5 min Zone 1	2 hr 20 min
	Wk 3	Swim 4x50 +60 Zone 1	Rest	Cycle/Run 30 min/10 min Zone 1	Swim 2x100 +60 Zone 1	Run 10 min Zone 1	Rest	Cycle/T-run 30 min/5 min Zone 1	2 hr
BASE 2	Wk 4	Swim 8x50 +60 Zone 1-2	Run 20 min Zone 1	Cycle 30 min Zone 1-2	Swim 4x100 +60 Zone 1	Run 15 min Zone 1-2	Rest	Cycle/T-run 45 min/5 min Zone 1	2 hr 40 min
	Wk 5	Swim 4x100 +30 Zone 1-2	Run 25 min Zone 1	Cycle 30 min Zones 1-2	Swim 2x200 +30 Zone 1-2	Run 15 min Zone 1-2	Rest	Cycle/T-run 60 min/5 min Zone 1	3 hr
	Wk 6	Swim 4x50 +60 Zone 1-2	Rest	Cycle/Run 30 min/10 min Zone 1-2	Swim 4x100 +60 Zone 1	Run 15 min Zone 1	Rest	Cycle/T-run 45 min/5 min Zone 1	2 hr 40 min
BASE 3	Wk 7	Swim 10x25 +20 Zone 1-2	Run 30 min Zone 1	Cycle 40 min Zone 2	Swim 1x200 +60 Zone 1	Run 15 min Zone 2	Rest	Cycle/T-run 60 min/10 min Zone 1	3 hr 20 min
	Wk 8	Swim 4x100 +20 Zone 1-2	Run 35 min Zone 1	Cycle 40 min Zone 2	Swim 6x100 +30 Zone 1	Run 15 min Zone 2	Rest	Cycle/T-run 75 min/10 min Zone 1	3 hr 40 min
	Wk 9	Swim 2x200 +30 Zone 1-2	Rest	Cycle/Run 40 min/15 min Zone 2	Swim 4x100 +60 Zone 1	Run 10 min Zone 1	Rest	Cycle/T-run 60 min/10 min Zone 1	3 hr
	Wk 10	Swim 8x50 +30 Zone 1-2	Run 40 min Zone 1	Cycle 40 min Zone 2	Swim 1x400 +60 Zone 1	Run 20 min Zone1-2	Rest	Cycle/T-run 75 min/10 min Zone 1	4 hr
PEAK	Wk 11	Swim 2x200 +30 Zone 1-2	Run 30 min Zone 1	Cycle 30 min Zone 2	Swim 4x100 +20 Zone 1	Run 15 min Zone 1-2	Rest	Cycle/T-run 40 min/5 min Zone 1	3 hr 20 min
RACE	Wk 12	Swim 4x100 +60 Zone 1	Rest	Cycle/Run 20 min/10 min Zone 1	Swim 4x100 +60 Zone 1	Run 10 min Zone 1-2	Cycle/Run 15 min/5 min Zone 1-2	RACE!	1 hr 40 min + race

Sprint distance: intermediate

		MON	TUES	WED	THURS	FRI	SAT	SUN	TOTAL TIME
BASE 1	**Wk 1**	**Swim** 8x50 +10 4x100 +20 Zone 1-2	**Run** 20 min Zone 2	**Cycle** 60 min Zone 2	**Swim** 4x100 +60 1x200 +60 Zone 1	**Run** 30 min Zone 2	Rest	**Cycle/T-run** 30 min/5 min Zone1-2	3 hr
	Wk 2	**Swim** 10x50 +10 4x100 +20 Zone 1	**Run** 25 min Zone 2	**Cycle** 60 min Zone 2	**Swim** 2x200 +60 4x100 +60 Zone 1-2	**Run** 35 min Zone 2	Rest	**Cycle/T-run** 45 min/5 min Zone 1-2	3 hr 20 min
	Wk 3	**Swim** 12x50 +10 4x100 +20 Zone 1-2	**Run** 30 min Zone 2	**Cycle** 60 min Zone 2	**Swim** 3x200 +30 4x100 +30 Zone 1-2	**Run** 40 min Zone 2	Rest	**Cycle/T-run** 60 min/5 min Zone 1-2	3 hr 40 min
	Wk 4	**Swim** 4x50 +20 2x100 +30 Zone 1-2	Rest	**Cycle/Run** 30 min/10 min Zone 2	**Swim** 3x200 +60 Zone 1	**Run** 35 min Zone 2	Rest	**Cycle/T-run** 45 min/5 min Zone 1-2	3 hr
BASE 2	**Wk 5**	**Swim** 8x50 +5 5x100 +20 Zone 1-2	**Run** 30 min Zone 2	**Cycle** 70 min Zone 2	**Swim** 1x200 +60 RP	**Run** 45 min Zone 2	Rest	**Cycle/T-run** 60 min/10 min Zone 1-2	4 hr
	Wk 6	**Swim** 10x50 +5 5x100 +20 Zone 1-2	**Run** 35 min Zone 2	**Cycle** 70 min Zone 2	**Swim** 5x100 +20 3x200 +20 Zone 1-2	**Run** 50 min Zone 2	Rest	**Cycle/T-run** 75 min/ 10 min Zone 1-2	4 hr 20 min
	Wk 7	**Swim** 12x50 +5 5x100 +20 Zone 1-2	**Run** 40 min Zone 2	**Cycle** 70 min Zone 2	**Swim** 4x100 +20 1x400 +60 Zone 1-2	**Run** 55 min Zone 2	Rest	**Cycle/T-run** 90 min/10 min Zone 1-2	4 hr 40 min
	Wk 8	**Swim** 6x50 +10 4x100 +30 Zone 1-2	Rest	**Cycle/Run** 45 min/20 min Zone 2	**Swim** 4x100 +30 2x200 +30 Zone 1	**Run** 50 min Zone 2	Rest	**Cycle/T-run** 75 min/10 min Zone 1-2	3 hr 20 min
BUILD	**Wk 9**	**Swim** 10x50 +10 alt 2x200 +20 Zone 1-2	**Run** 30 min Zone 4	**Cycle** 60 min Zone 1-4	**Swim** 4x100 +30 1x500 +60 Zone 2	**Run** 60 min Zone 2	Rest	**Cycle/T-run** 90 min/20 min Zone 1-2	5 hr
	Wk 10	**Swim** 12x50 +10 alt 2x200 +20 Zone 2	**Run** 30 min Zone 4	**Cycle** 60 min Zone 1-4	**Swim** 1x500 +60 RP	**Run** 65 min Zone 2	Rest	**Cycle/T-run** 105 min/20 min Zone 1-2	5 hr 20 min
PEAK	**Wk 11**	**Swim** 4x100 +10 2x200 +10 Zone 1-2	**Run** 20 min Zone 4	**Cycle** 60 min Zone 1-4	**Swim** 4x100 +30 2x200 +30 Zone 2	**Run** 70 min Zone 2	Rest	**Cycle/T-run** 60 min/10 min Zone 1-2	4 hr 40 min
RACE	**Wk 12**	**Swim** 2x100 +20 2x200 +20 Zone 1	**Run** 20 min Zone 1-2	**Cycle** 60 min Zone 1-2	**Swim** 1x400 +60 Zone 1	Rest	**Cycle/Run** 20 min/10 min Zone 1-4	RACE!	2 hr 40 min + race

Sprint distance: advanced

			MON	TUES	WED	THURS	FRI	SAT	SUN	TOTAL TIME
BASE 1	Wk 1	am	**Swim** 4x100 +10 3x200 +20 Zone 1-2	**Cycle** 60 min Zone 1-3	**Swim** 8x50 +10 8x50 +5 Zone 1-2	**Cycle** 60 min Zone 2	**Swim** 6x200 +30 Zone 1	Rest	**Cycle/T-run** 60 min/10 min Zone 1-2	7 hr
		pm	**Run** 30 min Zone 1	**X-train**	**Run** 30 min Zone 1-3	**X-train**	**Run** 40 min Zone 2	Rest		
	Wk 2	am	**Swim** 6x100 +10 3x200 +10 Zone 1-2	**Cycle** 75 min Zone 1-3	**Swim** 10x25 +5 6x100 +10 Zone 1-2	**Cycle** 60 min Zone 2	**Swim** 6x200 +20 Zone 1	Rest	**Cycle/T-run** 75 min/10 min Zone 1-2	7 hr 30 min
		pm	**Run** 30 min Zone 1	**X-train**	**Run** 40 min Zone 1-3	**X-train**	**Run** 45 min Zone 2	Rest		
	Wk 3	am	**Swim** 8x100 +10 3x200 +20 Zone 1-2	**Cycle** 90 min Zone 1-3	**Swim** 10x50 +10 10x50 +5 Zone 1-2	**Cycle** 60 min Zone 2	**Swim** 8x200 +20 Zone 1	Rest	**Cycle/T-run** 90 min/10 min Zone 1-2	8 hr
		pm	**Run** 30 min Zone 1	**X-train**	**Run** 50 min Zone 1-3	**X-train**	**Run** 50 min Zone 2	Rest		
	Wk 4	am	**Swim** 4x100 +10 3x200 +20 Zone 1-2	**Cycle/Run** 60 min/20 min Zone 1-2	**Swim** 12x25 +10 alt 4x100 +10 Zone 1-2	**Cycle** 40 min Zone 2	**Swim** 4x200 +60 Zone 2	Rest	**Cycle/T-run** 60 min/10 min Zone 1-2	7 hr
		pm		**X-train**	**Run** 30 min Zone 1	**X-train**	**Run** 30 min Zone 1	Rest		
BASE 2	Wk 5	am	**Swim** 6x100 +30 3x200 +30 Zone 1-2	**Cycle** 75 min Zone 1-3	**Swim** 10x50 +5 2x200 +10 Zone 1-2	**Cycle** 90 min Zone 1-2	**Swim** 4x400 +30 Zone 1	Rest	**Cycle/T-run** 90 min/10 min Zone 1-2	8 hr 30 min
		pm	**Run** 40 min Zone 1	**X-train**	**Run** 40 min Zone 1-3	**X-train**	**Run** 55 min Zone 2	Rest		
	Wk 6	am	**Swim** 6x100 +5 2x200 +10 Zone 1-2	**Cycle** 90 min Zone 1-3	**Swim** 12x50 +5 2x200 +10 Zone 1-2	**Cycle** 90 min Zone 1-2	**Swim** 4x500 +60 Zone 1	Rest	**Cycle/T-run** 120 min/10 min Zone 1-2	9 hr
		pm	**Run** 40 min Zone 1	**X-train**	**Run** 50 min Zone 1-3	**X-train**	**Run** 60 min Zone 2	Rest		
	Wk 7	am	**Swim** 8x100 +5 2x200 +10 Zone 1-2	**Cycle** 120 min Zone 1-3	**Swim** 14x50 +5 2x200 +10 Zone 1-2	**Cycle** 90 min Zone 1-2	**Swim** 4x500 +30 Zone 1	Rest	**Cycle/T-run** 135 min/10 min Zone 1-2	9 hr 30 min
		pm	**Run** 40 min Zone 1	**X-train**	**Run** 60 min Zone 1-3	**X-train**	**Run** 65 min Zone 1	Rest		
	Wk 8	am	**Swim** 6x100 +5 3x200 +10 Zone 1-2	**Cycle/Run** 90 min/30 min Zone 1-3	**Swim** 6x100 +10 1x200 +20 Zone 1	**Cycle** 60 min Zone 1-2	**Swim** 4x400 +60 Zone 1	Rest	**Cycle/T-run** 90 min/10 min Zone 1-2	8 hr 30 min
		pm		**X-train**	**Run** 40 min Zone 1	**X-train**	**Run** 40 min Zone 2	Rest		
BUILD	Wk 9	am	**Swim** 4x200 +10 2x200 +20 Zone 1-4	**Cycle** 90 min Zone 1-4	**Swim** 2x200 +20 RP 1x200 +20 Zone 1-4	**Cycle** 60 min Zone 2	**Swim** 1x500 +60 Zone 2	Rest	**Cycle/T-run** 90 min/20 min Zone 1-2	10 hr
		pm	**Run** 30 min Zone 2		**Run** 40 min Zone 4		**Run** 70 min Zone 1	Rest		
	Wk 10	am	**Swim** 6x100 +10 2x200 +10 Zone 1-4	**Cycle** 120 min Zone 1-4	**Swim** 3x200 +20 RP 1x200 +20	**Cycle** 90 min Zone 2	**Swim** 1x600 +60 Zone 2	Rest	**Cycle/T-run** 120 min/20 min Zone 1-2	10 hr 30 min
		pm	**Run** 30 min Zone 2		**Run** 50 min Zone 4		**Run** 75 min Zone 1	Rest		
PEAK	Wk 11	am	**Swim** 8x100 +10 3x200 +10 Zone 1-4	**Cycle** 90 min Zone 2	**Swim** 1x200 +20 RP 1x200 +20 Zone 2	**Cycle** 60 min Zone 2	**Swim** 1x500 Zone 1-2	Rest	**Cycle/T-run** 90 min/10 Zone 1-2	9 hr
		pm	**Run** 30 min Zone 2		**Run** 30 min Zone 4		**Run** 80 min Zone 1	Rest		
RACE	Wk 12	am	**Swim** 4x100 +20 1x200 +30 Zone 1	**Cycle/Run** 60 min/20 min Zone 2		**Cycle** 40 min Zone 1	**Swim** 2x200 +60 Zone 1	**Cycle/Run** 30 min/10 min Zone 2	RACE!	5 hr + race
		pm			**Run** 30 min Zone 1					

Olympic distance: unfit beginner

		MON	TUES	WED	THURS	FRI	SAT	SUN	TOTAL TIME
BASE 1	Wk 1	Swim 4x50 +30 Zone 1	Run 15 min Zone 1	Cycle 30 min Zone 1-2	Swim 2x100 +30 Zone 1	Run 15 min Zone 1-2	Rest	Cycle/T-run 60 min/5 min Zone 1	3 hr
	Wk 2	Swim 6x50 +30 Zone 1	Run 20 min Zone 1	Cycle 40 min Zone 1-2	Swim 3x100 +30 Zone 1	Run 15 min Zone 1-2	Rest	Cycle/T-run 70 min/5 min Zone 1	3 hr 30 min
	Wk 3	Swim 4x50 +60 Zone 1	Rest	Cycle/Run 30 min/10 min Zone 1-2	Swim 1x400 +60 Zone 1	Run 10 min Zone 1-2	Rest	Cycle/T-run 60 min/5 min Zone 1	3 hr
BASE 2	Wk 4	Swim 4x50 +20 Zone 1	Run 25 min Zone 1	Cycle 40 min Zone 1-2	Swim 4x100 +30 Zone 1	Run 20 min Zone 1-2	Rest	Cycle/T-run 70 min/5 min Zone 1	4 hr
	Wk 5	Swim 6x50 +20 Zone 1	Run 30 min Zone 1	Cycle 50 min Zone 1-2	Swim 5x100 +30 Zone 1	Run 20 min Zone 1-2	Rest	Cycle/T-run 80 min/ 5 min Zone 1	4 hr 30 min
	Wk 6	Swim 4x50 +30 Zone 1	Rest	Cycle/Run 40 min/20 min Zone 1-2	Swim 1x800 +60 Zone 1	Run 15 min Zone 1-2	Rest	Cycle/T-run 70 min/5 min Zone 1	4 hr
BASE 3	Wk 7	Swim 8x50 +10 Zone 1	Run 35 min Zone 1	Cycle 50 min Zone 1-2	Swim 6x100 +30 Zone 1	Run 25 min Zone 1-2	Rest	Cycle/T-run 80 min/5 min Zone 1	5 hr
	Wk 8	Swim 10x50 +10 Zone 1	Run 40 min Zone 1	Cycle 60 min Zone 1-2	Swim 3x200 +30 Zone 1	Run 25 min Zone 1-2	Rest	Cycle/T-run 90 min/5 min Zone 1	5 hr 30 min
	Wk 9	Swim 4x100 +30 Zone 1	Rest	Cycle/Run 50 min/ 30 min Zone 1-4	Swim 1x1000 +60 Zone 1	Run 15 min Zone 1-2	Rest	Cycle/T-run 80 min/5 min Zone 1	5 hr
	Wk 10	Swim 2x200 +30 Zone 1	Run 45 min Zone 1	Cycle 60 min Zone 1-4	Swim 2x500 +30 Zone 1	Run 20 min Zone 1-2	Rest	Cycle/T-run 60 min/5 min Zone 1	4 hr 30 min
PEAK	Wk 11	Swim 4x200 +30 Zone 1	Run 30 min Zone 1	Cycle 40 min Zone 1-4	Swim 1x400 +60 Zone 1	Run 15 min Zone 1-2	Rest	Cycle/T-run 40 min/5 min Zone 1	4 hr
RACE	Wk 12	Swim 4x200 +60 Zone 1	Run 20 min Zone 1	Cycle 40 min Zone 1-2	Swim 2x800 +60 Zone 1	Rest	Cycle/Run 30 min/10 min Zone 2	RACE!	3 hr + race

Olympic distance: fit beginner

		MON	TUES	WED	THURS	FRI	SAT	SUN	TOTAL TIME
BASE 1	Wk 1	**Swim** 4x50 +30 Zone 1	**Run** 20 min Zone 1-2	**Cycle** 45 min Zone 1-2	**Swim** 2x100 +30 Zone 1	**Run** 20 min Zone 2	Rest	**Cycle/T-run** 60 min/5 min Zone 1-2	3 hr
	Wk 2	**Swim** 6x50 +30 Zone 1	**Run** 25 min Zone 1-2	**Cycle** 45 min Zone 1-2	**Swim** 3x100 +30 Zone 1	**Run** 20 min Zone 2	Rest	**Cycle/T-run** 70 min/5 min Zone 1-2	3 hr 30 min
	Wk 3	**Swim** 4x50 +60 Zone 1	Rest	**Cycle/Run** 30 min/10 min Zone 1-2	**Swim** 1x500 +60 Zone 1	**Run** 15 min Zone 2	Rest	**Cycle/T-run** 60 min/5 min Zone 1-2	3 hr
BASE 2	Wk 4	**Swim** 8x50 +30 Zone 1	**Run** 30 min Zone 1-2	**Cycle** 60 min Zone 1-2	**Swim** 2x200 +30 Zone 1	**Run** 30 min Zone 2	Rest	**Cycle/T-run** 70 min/5 min Zone 1-2	4 hr 15 min
	Wk 5	**Swim** 10x50 +30 Zone 1	**Run** 35 min Zone 1-2	**Cycle** 60 min Zone 1-2	**Swim** 3x200 +30 Zone 1	**Run** 30 min Zone 2	Rest	**Cycle/T-run** 80 min/5 min Zone 1-2	4 hr 30 min
	Wk 6	**Swim** 8x50 +60 Zone 1	Rest	**Cycle/Run** 40 min/10 min Zone 1-2	**Swim** 1x800 +60 Zone 1	**Run** 20 min Zone 2	Rest	**Cycle/T-run** 70 min/5 min Zone 1-2	3 hr 30 min
BASE 3	Wk 7	**Swim** 6x100 +30 Zone 1	**Run** 40 min Zone 1-2	**Cycle** 60 min Zone 1-2	**Swim** 2x500 +20 Zone 1	**Run** 30 min Zone 2	Rest	**Cycle/T-run** 80 min/5 min Zone 1-2	5 hr
	Wk 8	**Swim** 4x200 +30 Zone 1	**Run** 45 min Zone 1-2	**Cycle** 60 min Zone 1-2	**Swim** 2x600 +20 Zone 1	**Run** 30 min Zone 2	Rest	**Cycle/T-run** 90 min/5 min Zone 1-2	5 hr 15 min
	Wk 9	**Swim** 6x100 +60 Zone 1	Rest	**Cycle/Run** 30 min/10 min Zone 1-3	**Swim** 1x1200 +60 Zone 1	**Run** 20 min Zone 2	Rest	**Cycle/T-run** 80 min/5 min Zone 1-2	4 hr 30
	Wk 10	**Swim** 6x100 +30 Zone 2	**Run** 50 min Zone 1-2	**Cycle** 60 min Zone 1-3	**Swim** 2x500 +10 Zone 1	**Run** 30 min Zone 1-3	Rest	**Cycle/T-run** 60 min /5 min Zone 1-2	5 hr
PEAK	Wk 11	**Swim** 3x200 +30 Zone 2	**Run** 40 min Zone 1-2	**Cycle** 60 min Zone 1-3	**Swim** 2x400 +10 Zone 1	**Run** 30 min Zone 1-3	Rest	**Cycle/T-run** 40 min/5 min Zone 1-2	4 hr
RACE	Wk 12	**Swim** 2x200 +20 Zone 2	Rest	**Cycle/Run** 30 min/10 min Zone 2	**Swim** 2x200 +20 Zone 1	Rest	**Cycle/Run** 30 min/10 min Zone 1-3	**RACE!**	2 hr 20 min + race

Olympic distance: intermediate

			MON	TUES	WED	THURS	FRI	SAT	SUN	TOTAL TIME
BASE 1	Wk 1	am	Swim 6x50 +20 6x50 +20 alt Zone 1-2	Cycle 60 min Zone 2	Swim 5x100 +20 5x100 +20 alt Zone 1-2	Cycle 60 min Zone 1-3	Swim 2x500 +30 Zone 1-2	Rest	Cycle/T-run 60 min/5 min Zone 1-2	5 hr 30 min
		pm	Run 30 min Zone 1	X-train	Run 40 min Zone 2	X-train	Run 30 min Zone 1-3	Rest		
	Wk 2	am	Swim 8x50 +20 8x50 +20 alt Zone 1-2	Cycle 60 min Zone 2	Swim 6x100 +20 6x100 +20 alt Zone 1-2	Cycle 60 min Zone 1-3	Swim 4x400 +20 Zone 1	Rest	Cycle/T-run 70 min/5 min Zone 1-2	6 hr
		pm	Run 30 min Zone 1	X-train	Run 45 min Zone 2	X-train	Run 30 min Zone 1-3	Rest		
	Wk 3	am	Swim 10x50 +20 10x50 +20 alt Zone 1-2	Cycle 60 min Zone 2	Swim 7x100 +20 7x100 +20 alt Zone 1-2	Cycle 60 min Zone 1-3	Swim 3x500 +20 Zone 1	Rest	Cycle/T-run 80 min/5 min Zone 1-2	6 hr 30 min
		pm	Run 30 min Zone 1	X-train	Run 50 min Zone 2	X-train	Run 30 min Zone 1-3	Rest		
	Wk 4	am	Swim 8x100 +30 Zone 1-2	Cycle/Run 40 min/20 min Zone 1-2	Swim 3x300 +30 Zone 1-2	Cycle 45 min Zone 1	Swim 1x1000 +60 Zone 1-2	Rest	Cycle/T-run 60 min/5 min Zone 1-2	4 hr 30 min
		pm		X-train	Run 30 min Zone 2	X-train	Run 20 min Zone 1	Rest		
BASE 2	Wk 5	am	Swim 6x50 +10 6x50 +10 alt Zone 1-2	Cycle 90 min Zone 2	Swim 5x100 +10 5x100 +10 alt Zone 1-2	Cycle 60 min Zone 1-3	Swim 1x1000 +60 RP	Rest	Cycle/T-run 80 min/5 min Zone 1-2	7 hr 15 min
		pm	Run 40 min Zone 1	X-train	Run 55 min Zone 2	X-train	Run 40 min Zone 1-3	Rest		
	Wk 6	am	Swim 8x50 +10 8x50 +10 Zone 1-2	Cycle 90 min Zone 2	Swim 6x100 +10 6x100 +10 alt Zone 1-2	Cycle 60 min Zone 1-3	Swim 3x600 +20 Zone 1	Rest	Cycle/T-run 90 min/5 min Zone 1-2	7 hr 45
		pm	Run 40 min Zone 1	X-train	Run 60 min Zone 2	X-train	Run 40 min Zone 1-3	Rest		
	Wk 7	am	Swim 10x50 +10 10x50 +10 alt Zone 1-2	Cycle 90 min Zone 2	Swim 7x100 +10 7x100 +10 alt Zone 1-2	Cycle 60 min Zone 1-3	Swim 4x500 +20 Zone 1	Rest	Cycle/T-run 100 min/5 min Zone 1-2	8 hr 15
		pm	Run 40 min Zone 1	X-train	Run 65 min Zone 2	X-train	Run 40 min Zone 1-3	Rest		
	Wk 8	am	Swim 3x200 +30 Zone 2	Cycle/Run 40 min/20 min Zone 1-4	Swim 4x300 +30 Zone 1-2	Cycle 45 min Zone 2	Swim 1x1200 +60 Zone 1-2	Rest	Cycle/T-run 60 min/10 min Zone 1-2	6 hr
		pm		X-train	Run 40 min Zone 2	X-train	Run 30 min Zone 2	Rest		
BUILD	Wk 9	am	Swim 4x200 +20 Zone 1-2	Cycle 60 min Zone 1-4	Swim 5x300 +20 Zone 1-2	Cycle 60 min Zone 1-4	Swim 1x1200 +60 RP	Rest	Cycle/T-run 100 min/10 min Zone 1-2	8 hr
		pm	Run 30 min Zone 1		Run 70 min Zone 2		Run 30 min Zone 1-4	Rest		
	Wk 10	am	Swim 3x200 +20 Zone 1-2	Cycle 60 min Zone 1-4	Swim 4x300 +20 Zone 1-2	Cycle 60 min Zone 1-4	Swim 1x1500 +60 Zone 1-2	Rest	Cycle/T-run 110 min/10 min Zone 1-2	8 hr 30 min
		pm	Run 30 min Zone 1		Run 75 min Zone 2		Run 30 min Zone 1-4	Rest		
PEAK	Wk 11	am	Swim 2x200 +20 Zone 1-2	Cycle 60 min Zone 1-4	Swim 3x300 +20 Zone 1-2	Cycle 40 min Zone 1-4	Swim 2x500 +30 Zone 1-2	Rest	Cycle/T-run 90 min/10 min Zone 1-2	8 hr
		pm	Run 30 min Zone 1		Run 80 min Zone 2		Run 30 min Zone 1-4	Rest		
RACE	Wk 12	am	Swim 2x200 +30 Zone 1-2	Cycle/Run 30 min/10 min Zone 1-2	Swim 2x300 +20 Zone 1-2	Cycle 60 min Zone 2	Swim 1x600 +60 Zone 1-2	Cycle/Run 30 min/10 min Zone 1-4	RACE!	4 hr 15 min + race
		pm			Run 30 min Zone 2					

Olympic distance: advanced

			MON	TUES	WED	THURS	FRI	SAT	SUN	TOTAL TIME
BASE 1	Wk 1	am	Swim 4x100 +20 2x200 +30 Zone 2	Cycle 60 min Zone 1-3	Swim 10x25 +10 10x50 +10 alt Zone 1-2	Cycle 60 min Zone 2	Swim 5x200 +30 Zone 1-2	Rest	Cycle/T-run 90 min/5 min Zone 1-2	7 hr 30 min
		pm	Run 30 min Zone 1	X-train	Run 40 min Zone 1-2	X-train	Run 20 min Zone 1-3	Rest		
	Wk 2	am	Swim 6x100 +20 2x200 +30 Zone 2	Cycle 75 min Zone 1-3	Swim 12x25 +10 12x50 +10 alt Zone 1-2	Cycle 75 min Zone 2	Swim 6x200 +30 Zone 1-2	Rest	Cycle/T-run 105 min/5 min Zone 1-2	8 hr
		pm	Run 30 min Zone 1	X-train	Run 50 min Zone 1-2	X-train	Run 30 min Zone 1-3	Rest		
	Wk 3	am	Swim 6x100 +20 2x200 +30 Zone 2	Cycle 75 min Zone 1-3	Swim 12x25 +10 12x50 +10 alt Zone 1-2	Cycle 75 min Zone 2	Swim 6x200 +30 Zone 1-2	Rest	Cycle/T-run 120 min/5 min Zone 1-2	8 hr
		pm	Run 30 min Zone 1	X-train	Run 50 min Zone 1-2	X-train	Run 30 min Zone 1-3	Rest		
	Wk 4	am	Swim 4x100 +20 2x200 +30 Zone 2	Cycle/Run 60 min/20 min Zone 1-3	Swim 10x25 +10 10x50 +10 Zone 1-2	Cycle 60 min Zone 2	Swim 5x200 +30 Zone 1-2	Rest	Cycle/T-run 90 min/5 min Zone 1-2	7 hr 30 min
		pm		X-train	Run 40 min Zone 1-2	X-train	Run 20 min Zone 1-3	Rest		
BASE 2	Wk 5	am	Swim 6x100 +10 2x200 +20 Zone 2	Cycle 75 min Zone 1-3	Swim 12x25 +10 12x50 +10 alt Zone 1-2	Cycle 75 min Zone 2	Swim 6x200 +30 Zone 1-2	Rest	Cycle/T-run 105 min/5 min Zone 1-2	8 hr
		pm	Run 40 min Zone 1	X-train	Run 50 min Zone 1-2	X-train	Run 30 min Zone 1-3	Rest		
	Wk 6	am	Swim 6x100 +10 2x200 +20 Zone 2	Cycle 75 min Zone 1-3	Swim 12x25 +10 12x50 +10 alt Zone 1-2	Cycle 75 min Zone 2	Swim 6x200 +30 Zone 1-2	Rest	Cycle/T-run 120 min/5 min Zone 1-2	8 hr
		pm	Run 40 min Zone 1	X-train	Run 50 min Zone 1-2	X-train	Run 30 min Zone 1-3	Rest		
	Wk 7	am	Swim 4x100 +10 2x200 +20 Zone 2	Cycle 60 min Zone 1-3	Swim 10x25 +10 10x50 +10 Zone 1-2	Cycle 60 min Zone 2	Swim 5x200 +30 Zone 1-2	Rest	Cycle/T-run 135 min/5 min Zone 1-2	7 hr 30 min
		pm	Run 40 min Zone 1	X-train	Run 40 min Zone 1-2	X-train	Run 20 min Zone 1-3	Rest		
	Wk 8	am	Swim 6x100 +20 2x200 +30 Zone 2	Cycle/Run 80 min/30 min Zone 1-3	Swim 12x25 +10 12x50 +10 alt Zone 1-2	Cycle 75 min Zone 2	Swim 6x200 +30 Zone 1-2	Rest	Cycle/T-run 105 min/5 min Zone 1-2	8 hr
		pm		X-train	Run 50 min Zone 1-2	X-train	Run 30 min Zone 1-3	Rest		
BUILD	Wk 9	am	Swim 6x100 +20 2x200 +30 Zone 2	Cycle 75 min Zone 1-4	Swim 12x25 +10 12x50 +10 alt Zone 1-2	Cycle 75 min Zone 2	Swim 6x200 +30 Zone 1-2	Rest	Cycle/T-run 120 min/5 min Zone 1-2	8 hr
		pm	Run 40 min Zone 2	X-train or rest	Run 50 min Zone 1-2	X-train or rest	Run 30 min Zone 1-4	Rest		
	Wk 10	am	Swim 4x100 +20 2x200 +30 Zone 1	Cycle 60 min Zone 1-4	Swim 10x25 +10 10x50 +10 Zone 1-2	Cycle 60 min Zone 2	Swim 5x200 +30 Zone 1-2	Rest	Cycle/T-run 90 min/5 min Zone 1-2	7 hr 30 min
		pm	Run 40 min Zone 1	X-train or rest	Run 40 min Zone 1-2	X-train rest	Run 20 min Zone 1-4	Rest		
PEAK	Wk 11	am	Swim 6x100 +20 2x200 +30 Zone 2	Cycle 75 min Zone 1-4	Swim 12x25 +10 12x50 +10 alt Zone 1-2	Cycle 75 min Zone 2	Swim 6x200 +30 Zone 1-2	Rest	Cycle/T-run 60 min/5 min Zone 1-2	8 hr
		pm	Run 40 min Zone 1	X-train or rest	Run 50 min Zone 1-2	X-train or rest	Run 30 min Zone 1-4	Rest		
RACE	Wk 12	am	Swim 6x100 +20 2x200 +30 Zone 2	Cycle/Run 30 min/10 min Zone 1-4	Swim 12x25 +10 12x50 +10 Zone 1-2	Cycle 75 min Zone 2	Swim 6x200 +30 Zone 1-2	Cycle/Run 30 min/10 min Zone 1-4	RACE!	8 hr
		pm		X-train or rest	Run 50 min Zone 1-2	X-train or rest				

Half-Ironman: novice

			MON	TUES	WED	THURS	FRI	SAT	SUN	TOTAL TIME
BASE 1	Wk 1	am	Swim 30 min Zone 1-2	Cycle 60 min Zone 2	Swim 30 min Zone 1-2	Cycle 60 min Zone 1-3	Swim 40 min Zone 1	Rest	Cycle/T-run 90 min/5 min Zone 1-2	7 hr
		pm	Run 20 min Zone 1		Run 60 min Zone 2		Run 20 min Zone 1-3	Rest		
	Wk 2	am	Swim 30 min Zone 1-2	Cycle 60 min Zone 2	Swim 30 min Zone 1-2	Cycle 70 min Zone 1-3	Swim 40 min Zone 1	Rest	Cycle/T-run 105 min/5 min Zone 1-2	7 hr 30 min
		pm	Run 25 min Zone 1		Run 65 min Zone 2		Run 25 min Zone 1-3	Rest		
	Wk 3	am	Swim 30 min Zone 1-2	Cycle 60 min Zone 2	Swim 30 min Zone 1-2	Cycle 80 min Zone 1-3	Swim 40 min Zone 1	Rest	Cycle/T-run 120 min/5 min Zone 1-2	8 hr
		pm	Run 30 min Zone 1		Run 70 min Zone 2		Run 30 min Zone 1-3	Rest		
	Wk 4	am	Swim 30 min Zone 1-2	Cycle/Run 40 min/15 min Zone 1-3	Swim 30 min Zone 1-2	Cycle 60 min Zone 1-3	Swim 40 min Zone 1	Rest	Cycle/T-run 90 min/5 min Zone 1-2	6 hr 30 min
		pm			Run 20 min Zone 1-3		Run 20 min Zone 1-3	Rest		
BASE 2	Wk 5	am	Swim 40 min Zone 1-2	Cycle 75 min Zone 2	Swim 40 min Zone 1-2	Cycle 60 min Zone 1-3	Swim 1x500 +60 RP	Rest	Cycle/T-run 120 min/5 min Zone 1-2	8 hr 30
		pm	Run 30 min Zone 1		Run 75 min Zone 2		Run 30 min Zone 1-3	Rest		
	Wk 6	am	Swim 40 min Zone 1-2	Cycle 75 min Zone 2	Swim 40 min Zone 1-2	Cycle 70 min Zone 1-3	Swim 50 min Zone 1	Rest	Cycle/T-run 135 min/5 min Zone 1-2	9 hr
		pm	Run 35 min Zone 1		Run 80 min Zone 2		Run 35 min Zone 1-3	Rest		
	Wk 7	am	Swim 40 min Zone 1-2	Cycle 75 min Zone 2	Swim 40 min Zone 1-2	Cycle 80 min Zone 1-3	Swim 50 min Zone 1	Rest	Cycle/T-run 150 min/5 min Zone 1-2	9 hr 30 min
		pm	Run 40 min Zone 1		Run 85 min Zone 2		Run 40 min Zone 1-3	Rest		
	Wk 8	am	Swim 40 min Zone 1-2	Cycle/Run 60 min/20 min Zone 1-3	Swim 40 min Zone 1-2	Cycle 60 min Zone 1	Swim 50 min Zone 1	Rest	Cycle/T-run 135 min/5 min Zone 1-2	7 hr 30 min
		pm			Run 60 min Zone 2		Run 30 min Zone 1-3	Rest		

			MON	TUES	WED	THURS	FRI	SAT	SUN	TOTAL TIME
BASE 3	Wk 9	am	Swim 50 min Zone 1-2	Cycle 90 min Zone 2	Swim 50 min Zone 1-2	Cycle 60 min Zone 1-3	Swim 1x1000 +60 RP	Rest	Cycle/T-run 150 min/10 min Zone 1-2	10 hr
		pm	Run 40 min Zone 1		Run 90 min Zone 2		Run 40 min Zone 1-3	Rest		
	Wk 10	am	Swim 50 min Zone 1-2	Cycle 90 min Zone 2	Swim 50 min Zone 1-2	Cycle 70 min Zone 1-3	Swim 60 min Zone 1	Rest	Cycle/T-run 165 min/10 min Zone 1-2	10 hr 30 min
		pm	Run 45 min Zone 1		Run 95 min Zone 2		Run 45 min Zone 1-3	Rest		
	Wk 11	am	Swim 50 min Zone 1-2	Cycle 90 min Zone 2	Swim 50 min Zone 1-2	Cycle 80 min Zone 1-3	Swim 60 min Zone 1	Rest	Cycle/T-run 180 min/10 min Zone 1-2	11 hr
		pm	Run 50 min Zone 1		Run 100 min Zone 2		Run 50 min Zone 1-3	Rest		
	Wk 12	am	Swim 50 min Zone 1-2	Cycle/Run 80 min/25 min Zone 1-3	Swim 50 min Zone 1-2	Cycle 60 min Zone 1	Swim 1x1500 +60 RP	Rest	Cycle/T-run 165 min/5 min Zone 1-2	9 hr 30 min
		pm			Run 80 min Zone 2		Run 30 min Zone 1-3	Rest		
BUILD	Wk 13	am	Swim 60 min Zone 1-2	Cycle/Run 60 min/20 min Zone 1-4	Swim 60 min Zone 1-2	Cycle 60 min Zone 2	Swim 70 min Zone 1	Rest	Cycle/T-run 165 min/5 min Zone 1-2	10 hr 30
		pm			Run 105 min Zone 2		Run 30 min Zone 1-4	Rest		
	Wk 14	am	Swim 60 min Zone 1-2	Cycle/Run 50 min/15 min Zone 1-4	Swim 60 min Zone 1-2	Cycle 60 min Zone 2	Swim 1x1000 +60 RP	Rest	Cycle/T-run 120 min/5 min Zone 1-2	9 hr
		pm			Run 110 min Zone 2		Run 25 min Zone 1-4	Rest		
PEAK	Wk 15	am	Swim 40 min Zone 1-2	Cycle/Run 40 min/10 min Zone 1-4	Swim 40 min Zone 1-2	Cycle 50 min Zone 2	Swim 1x800 +60 Zone 1	Rest	Cycle/T-run 90 min/5 min Zone 1-2	6 hr
		pm			Run 40 min Zone 2		Run 20 min Zone 1-4	Rest		
RACE	Wk 16	am	Swim 30 min Zone 1	Cycle/Run 30 min/10 min Zone 2	Swim 30 min Zone 1	Cycle 30 min Zone 1	Swim 1x400 +60 RP	Cycle/Run 30 min/10 Zone 1-4	RACE!	3 hr + race
		pm			Run 30 min Zone 1					

Half-Ironman: intermediate

			MON	TUES	WED	THURS	FRI	SAT	SUN	TOTAL TIME
BASE 1	Wk 1	am	Swim 40 min Zone 1	Cycle 60 min Zone 2	Swim 40 min Zone 2	Cycle 60 min Zone 1-3	Swim 60 min Zone 1	Rest	Cycle/T-run 90 min/5 min Zone 1-2	7 hr 30 min
		pm	Run 40 min Zone 1		Run 40 min Zone 2		Run 20 min Zone 1-3	Rest		
	Wk 2	am	Swim 40 min Zone 1	Cycle 70 min Zone 2	Swim 40 min Zone 2	Cycle 70 min Zone 1-3	Swim 60 min Zone 1	Rest	Cycle/T-run 105 min/5 min Zone 1-2	8 hr 15 min
		pm	Run 50 min Zone 1		Run 50 min Zone 2		Run 25 min Zone 1-3	Rest		
	Wk 3	am	Swim 40 min Zone 1	Cycle 80 min Zone 2	Swim 40 min Zone 2	Cycle 80 min Zone 1-3	Swim 60 min Zone 1	Rest	Cycle/T-run 120 min/5 min Zone 1-2	9 hr
		pm	Run 60 min Zone 1		Run 60 min Zone 2		Run 30 min Zone 1-3	Rest		
	Wk 4	am	Swim 30 min Zone 1	Cycle/Run 60 min/20 min Zone 1-3	Swim 30 min Zone 1	Cycle 60 min Zone 2	Swim 40 min Zone 1	Rest	Cycle/T-run 80 min/5 min Zone 1-2	6 hr 30 min
		pm			Run 20 min Zone 2		Run 20 min Zone 1-3	Rest		
BASE 2	Wk 5	am	Swim 50 min Zone 1	Cycle 60 min Zone 2	Swim 50 min Zone 2	Cycle 60 min Zone 1-3	Swim 1x1000 +60 RP Zone 1	Rest	Cycle/T-run 120 min/5 min Zone 1-2	9 hr 15 min
		pm	Run 40 min Zone 1		Run 70 min Zone 2		Run 30 min Zone 1-3	Rest		
	Wk 6	am	Swim 50 min Zone 1	Cycle 70 min Zone 2	Swim 50 min Zone 2	Cycle 70 min Zone 1-3	Swim 70 min Zone 1	Rest	Cycle/T-run 135 min/5 min Zone 1-2	9 hr 45 min
		pm	Run 50 min Zone 1		Run 80 min Zone 2		Run 35 min Zone 1-3	Rest		
	Wk 7	am	Swim 50 min Zone 1	Cycle 80 min Zone 2	Swim 50 min Zone 2	Cycle 80 min Zone 1-3	Swim 70 min Zone 1	Rest	Cycle/T-run 150 min/5 min Zone 1-2	10 hr 15 min
		pm	Run 60 min Zone 1		Run 90 min Zone 2		Run 40 min Zone 1-3	Rest		
	Wk 8	am	Swim 40 min Zone 1	Cycle/Run 80 min/30 min Zone 1-3	Swim 40 min Zone 2	Cycle 60 min Zone 1-3	Swim 50 min Zone 1	Rest	Cycle/T-run 75 min/5 min Zone 1-2	8 hr
		pm			Run 90 min Zone 2		Run 30 min Zone 1-3	Rest		

			MON	TUES	WED	THURS	FRI	SAT	SUN	TOTAL TIME
BASE 3	Wk 9	am	Swim 60 min Zone 1	Cycle 60 min Zone 2	Swim 60 min Zone 2	Cycle 60 min Zone 1-3	Swim 1x1200 +60 RP	Rest	Cycle/T-run 150 min/10 min Zone 1-2	10 hr 30
		pm	Run 40 min Zone 1		Run 100 min Zone 2		Run 40 min Zone 1-3	Rest		
	Wk 10	am	Swim 60 min Zone 1	Cycle 70 min Zone 2	Swim 60 min Zone 2	Cycle 70 min Zone 1-3	Swim 70 min Zone 1	Rest	Cycle/T-run 165 min/10 min Zone 1-2	11 hr
		pm	Run 40 min Zone 1		Run 110 min Zone 2		Run 45 min Zone 1-3	Rest		
	Wk 11	am	Swim 60 min Zone 1	Cycle 80 min Zone 2	Swim 60 min Zone 2	Cycle 80 min Zone 1-3	Swim 70 min Zone 1	Rest	Cycle/T-run 180 min/10 min Zone 1-2	11 hr 30 min
		pm	Run 40 min Zone 1		Run 120 min Zone 2		Run 50 min Zone 1-3	Rest		
	Wk 12	am	Swim 50 min Zone 1	Cycle/Run 60 min/20 min Zone 1-4	Swim 50 min Zone 2	Cycle 60 min Zone 2	Swim 60 min Zone 1	Rest	Cycle/T-run 105 min/5 min Zone 1-2	8 hr
		pm			Run 90 min Zone 1		Run 40 min Zone 1-3	Rest		
BUILD	Wk 13	am	Swim 40 min Zone 1	Cycle 60 min Zone 1-4	Swim 40 min Zone 2	Cycle 60 min Zone 1-4	Swim 1x1500 +60 RP	Rest	Cycle/T-run 180 min/5 min Zone 1-2	10 hr
		pm	Run 30 min Zone 1		Run 120 min Zone 2		Run 40 min Zone 1-4	Rest		
	Wk 14	am	Swim 40 min Zone 1	Cycle/Run 40 min/15 min Zone 1-4	Swim 40 min Zone 2	Cycle 50 min Zone 1-4	Swim 50 min Zone 1	Rest	Cycle/T-run 90 min/5 min Zone 1-2	8 hr
		pm			Run 90 min Zone 2		Run 30 min Zone 1-4	Rest		
PEAK	Wk 15	am	Swim 30 min Zone 1	Cycle 40 min Zone 1-4	Swim 30 min Zone 2	Cycle 40 min Zone 1-4	Swim 1x500 +60 RP	Rest	Cycle/T-run 60 min/5 min Zone 1-2	6 hr
		pm	Run 30 min Zone 1		Run 60 min Zone 2		Run 20 min Zone 1-4	Rest		
RACE	Wk 16	am	Swim 30 min Zone 1-2	Cycle/Run 30 min/10 min Zone 2	Swim 30 min Zone 2	Rest	Swim 30 min Zone 1	Cycle/Run 30 min/10 min Zone 1-4	RACE!	3 hr + race
		pm				Rest				

Half-Ironman: advanced

			MON	TUES	WED	THURS	FRI	SAT	SUN	TOTAL TIME
BASE 1	Wk 1	am	Swim 40 min Zone 1-2	Cycle 60 min Zone 2	Swim 40 min Zone 2	Cycle 60 min Zone 1-3	Swim 60 min Zone 1	Rest	Cycle/T-run 120 min/5 min Zone 1-2	8 hr 40 min
		pm	Run 40 min Zone 1	X-train	Run 40 min Zone 2	X-train	Run 40 min Zone 1-3	Rest		
	Wk 2	am	Swim 40 min Zone 1-2	Cycle 70 min Zone 2	Swim 40 min Zone 2	Cycle 60 min Zone 1-3	Swim 60 min Zone 1	Rest	Cycle/T-run 135 min/5 min Zone 1-2	9 hr
		pm	Run 50 min Zone 1	X-train	Run 50 min Zone 2	X-train	Run 40 min Zone 1-3	Rest		
	Wk 3	am	Swim 40 min Zone 1-2	Cycle 80 min Zone 2	Swim 40 min Zone 2	Cycle 60 min Zone 1-3	Swim 60 min Zone 1	Rest	Cycle/T-run 150 min/5 min Zone 1-2	9 hr 45 min
		pm	Run 60 min Zone 1	X-train	Run 60 min Zone 2	X-train	Run 40 min Zone 1-3	Rest		
	Wk 4	am	Swim 30 min Zone 1-2	Cycle/Run 60 min/20 min Zone 1-3	Swim 30 min Zone 2	Cycle 40 min Zone 2	Swim 40 min Zone 1	Rest	Cycle/T-run 120 min/5 min Zone 1-2	7 hr
		pm		X-train	Run 40 min Zone 2	X-train	Run 20 min Zone 1-3	Rest		
BASE 2	Wk 5	am	Swim 50 min Zone 1-2	Cycle 60 min Zone 2	Swim 50 min Zone 2	Cycle 60 min Zone 1-3	Swim 30 min RP	Rest	Cycle/T-run 150 min/5 min Zone 1-2	9 hr 45 min
		pm	Run 40 min Zone 1	X-train	Run 60 min Zone 2	X-train	Run 50 min Zone 1-3	Rest		
	Wk 6	am	Swim 50 min Zone 1-2	Cycle 70 min Zone 2	Swim 50 min Zone 2	Cycle 60 min Zone 1-3	Swim 70 min Zone 1	Rest	Cycle/T-run 165 min/5 min Zone 1-2	10 hr 30 min
		pm	Run 50 min Zone 1	X-train	Run 70 min Zone 2	X-train	Run 50 min Zone 1-3	Rest		
	Wk 7	am	Swim 50 min Zone 1-2	Cycle 80 min Zone 2	Swim 50 min Zone 2	Cycle 60 min Zone 1-3	Swim 70 min Zone 1	Rest	Cycle/T-run 180 min/5 min Zone 1-2	11 hr 15 min
		pm	Run 60 min Zone 1	X-train	Run 80 min Zone 2	X-train	Run 50 min Zone 1-3	Rest		
	Wk 8	am	Swim 40 min Zone 1-2	Cycle/Run 90 min/30 min Zone 1-3	Swim 40 min Zone 2	Cycle 40 min Zone 1-3	Swim 50 min Zone 1	Rest	Cycle/T-run 120 min/5 min Zone 1-2	11 hr 45 min
		pm		X-train	Run 50 min Zone 2	X-train	Run 40 min Zone 1-3	Rest		

			MON	TUES	WED	THURS	FRI	SAT	SUN	TOTAL TIME
BASE 3	Wk 9	am	Swim 40 min Zone 1-2	Cycle 60 min Zone 1-4	Swim 40 min Zone 2	Cycle 60 min Zone 1	Swim 45 min RP	Rest	Cycle/T-run 180 min/10 min Zone 1-2	10 hr 15 min
		pm	Run 40 min Zone 1		Run 80 min Zone 2		Run 40 min Zone 2	Rest		
	Wk 10	am	Swim 40 min Zone 1-2	Cycle/Run 80 min/40 min Zone 1-4	Swim 40 min Zone 2	Cycle 60 min Zone 1	Swim 60 min Zone 1	Rest	Cycle/T-run 195 min/10 min Zone 1-2	11 hr
		pm			Run 90 min Zone 2		Run 40 min Zone 2	Rest		
	Wk 11	am	Swim 40 min Zone 1-2	Cycle 60 min Zone 2	Swim 40 min Zone 2	Cycle 60 min Zone 1	Swim 60 min RP	Rest	Cycle/T-run 210 min/10 min Zone 1-2	11 hr
		pm	Run 40 min Zone 1		Run 100 min Zone 2		Run 40 min Zone 2	Rest		
	Wk 12	am	Swim 30 min Zone 1-2	Cycle/Run 100 min/60 min Zone 1-4	Swim 30 min Zone 2	Cycle 40 min Zone 1	Swim 40 min Zone 1	Rest	Cycle/T-run 150 min/10 min Zone 1-2	9 hr
		pm			Run 80 min Zone 2		Run 20 min Zone 2	Rest		
BUILD	Wk 13	am	Swim 30 min Zone 1-2	Cycle 60 min Zone 2	Swim 30 min Zone 2	Cycle 60 min Zone 1	Swim 45 min RP	Rest	Cycle/T-run 210 min/5 min Zone 1-2	10 hr
		pm	Run 30 min Zone 1		Run 100 min Zone 2		Run 30 min Zone 1-4	Rest		
	Wk 14	am	Swim 30 min Zone 1-2	Cycle/Run 60 min/20 min Zone 1-4	Swim 30 min Zone 2	Cycle 40 min Zone 1	Swim 30 min Zone 1	Rest	Cycle/T-run 150 min/5 min Zone 1-2	8 hr 30 min
		pm			Run 110 min Zone 2		Run 30 min Zone 1-4	Rest		
PEAK	Wk 15	am	Swim 30 min Zone 1-2	Cycle 40 min Zone 1-4	Swim 30 min Zone 2	Cycle 40 min Zone 1	Swim 30 min RP	Rest	Cycle/T-run 90 min/5 min Zone 1-2	7 hr
		pm	Run 30 min Zone 1		Run 80 min Zone 2		Run 30 min Zone 1-4	Rest		
RACE	Wk 16	am	Swim 20 min Zone 1	Cycle/Run 30 min/10 min Zone 1-4	Swim 20 min Zone 2	Cycle 30 min Zone 1	Swim 20 min Zone 1	Cycle/Run 30 min/10 min Zone 1-4	RACE!	3 hr + race
		pm								

Ironman: to finish

			MON	TUES	WED	THURS	FRI	SAT	SUN	TOTAL TIME
BASE 1	Wk 1	am	Swim 20 min Zone 1	Cycle 60 min Zone 2	Swim 20 min Zone 1	Cycle 45 min Zone 1	Swim 20 min Zone 1	Rest	Cycle 75 min Zone 1-2	4 hr 30 min
		pm	Run 20 min Zone 1		Run 45 min Zone 2		Run 20 min Zone 1-2	Rest		
	Wk 2	am	Swim 20 min Zone 1	Cycle 60 min Zone 2	Swim 20 min Zone 1	Cycle 45 min Zone 1	Swim 20 min Zone 1	Rest	Cycle 90 min Zone 1-2	5 hr
		pm	Run 25 min Zone 1		Run 50 min Zone 2		Run 25 min Zone 1-2	Rest		
	Wk 3	am	Swim 20 min Zone 1	Cycle 60 min Zone 2	Swim 20 min Zone 1	Cycle 45 min Zone 1	Swim 20 min Zone 1	Rest	Cycle 105 min Zone 1-2	5 hr 30 min
		pm	Run 30 min Zone 1		Run 55 min Zone 2		Run 30 min Zone 1-2	Rest		
	Wk 4	am	Swim 20 min Zone 1	Cycle/Run 40 min/10 min Zone 2	Swim 20 min Zone 2	Cycle 45 min Zone 1	Swim 20 min Zone 1	Rest	Rest	3 hr 30 min
		pm			Run 30 min Zone 2		Run 15 min Zone 1-2	Rest	Rest	
BASE 2	Wk 5	am	Swim 30 min Zone 1	Cycle 75 min Zone 2	Swim 30 min Zone 1	Cycle 60 min Zone 1	Swim 1x800 +60 RP	Rest	Cycle 120 min Zone 1-2	6 hr 15 min
		pm	Run 20 min Zone 1		Run 60 min Zone 2		Run 20 min Zone 1-2	Rest		
	Wk 6	am	Swim 30 min Zone 1	Cycle 75 min Zone 2	Swim 30 min Zone 1	Cycle 60 min Zone 1	Swim 30 min Zone 1	Rest	Cycle 135 min Zone 1-2	6 hr 45 min
		pm	Run 25 min Zone 2		Run 65 min Zone 2		Run 25 min Zone 1-2	Rest		
	Wk 7	am	Swim 30 min Zone 1	Cycle 75 min Zone 2	Swim 30 min Zone 1	Cycle 60 min Zone 1	Swim 30 min Zone 1	Rest	Cycle 150 min Zone 1-2	7 hr 15 min
		pm	Run 30 min Zone 1		Run 70 min Zone 2		Run 30 min Zone 1-2	Rest		
	Wk 8	am	Swim 20 min Zone 1	Cycle/Run 60 min/20 min Zone 2	Swim 20 min Zone 1	Cycle 45 min Zone 1	Swim 20 min Zone 1	Rest	Rest	5 hr 30 min
		pm			Run 40 min Zone 2		Run 15 min Zone 1-2	Rest	Rest	
BASE 3	Wk 9	am	Swim 40 min Zone 1	Cycle 90 min Zone 2	Swim 40 min Zone 1	Cycle 75 min Zone 1	Swim 1x1600 +60 RP	Rest	Cycle 165 min Zone 1-2	8 hr 15 min
		pm	Run 30 min Zone 1		Run 75 min Zone 2		Run 30 min Zone 1-2	Rest		
	Wk 10	am	Swim 40 min Zone 1	Cycle 90 min Zone 2	Swim 40 min Zone 1	Cycle 75 min Zone 1	Swim 40 min Zone 1	Rest	Cycle 180 min Zone 1-2	8 hr 45 min
		pm	Run 35 min Zone 1		Run 80 min Zone 2		Run 35 min Zone 1-2	Rest		
	Wk 11	am	Swim 40 min Zone 1	Cycle 90 min Zone 2	Swim 40 min Zone 1	Cycle 75 min Zone 1	Swim 40 min Zone 1	Rest	Cycle 195 min Zone 1-2	9 hr 30
		pm	Run 40 min Zone 1		Run 85 min Zone 2		Run 40 min Zone 1-2	Rest		
	Wk 12	am	Swim 30 min Zone 1	Cycle/Run 80 min/30 min Zone 2	Swim 30 min Zone 1	Cycle 60 min Zone 1	Swim 30 min Zone 1	Rest	Rest	6 hr
		pm			Run 40 min Zone 2		Run 30 min Zone 1-2	Rest	Rest	

	Wk		MON	TUES	WED	THURS	FRI	SAT	SUN	TOTAL TIME
BUILD 1	Wk 13	am	Swim 50 min Zone 1	Cycle 105 min Zone 2	Swim 50 min Zone 1	Cycle 90 min Zone 1	Swim 3x800 +20 Zone 1	Rest	Cycle/T-run 210 min/5 min Zone 1-2	10 hr 30 min
		pm	Run 45 min Zone 1		Run 90 min Zone 2		Run 45 min Zone 1-2	Rest		
	Wk 14	am	Swim 50 min Zone 1	Cycle 105 min Zone 2	Swim 50 min Zone 1	Cycle 90 min Zone 1	Swim 50 min Zone 1	Rest	Cycle/T-run 225 min/5 min Zone 1-2	11 hr 15 min
		pm	Run 50 min Zone 1		Run 95 min Zone 2		Run 50 min Zone 1-2	Rest		
	Wk 15	am	Swim 50 min Zone 1	Cycle 105 min Zone 2	Swim 50 min Zone 1	Cycle 90 min Zone 1	Swim 50 min Zone 1	Rest	Cycle/T-run 240 min/5 min Zone 1-2	11 hr 45 min
		pm	Run 55 min Zone 1		Run 100 min Zone 2		Run 55 min Zone 1-2	Rest		
	Wk 16	am	Swim 40 min Zone 1	Cycle/Run 100 min/40 min Zone 2	Swim 40 min Zone 1	Cycle 60 min Zone 1	Swim 40 min Zone 1	Rest	Rest	6 hr 30 min
		pm			Run 75 min Zone 2		Run 45 min Zone 1-2	Rest	Rest	
BUILD 2	Wk 17	am	Swim 60 min Zone 1	Cycle 90 min Zone 2	Swim 60 min Zone 1	Cycle 75 min Zone 1	Swim 60 min Zone 1	Rest	Cycle/T-run 255 min/5 min Zone 1-2	12 hr
		pm	Run 60 min Zone 1		Run 105 min Zone 2		Run 60 min Zone 1-2	Rest		
	Wk 18	am	Swim 60 min Zone 1	Cycle/Run 120 min/50 min Zone 2	Swim 60 min Zone 1	Cycle 75 min Zone 1	Swim 60 min Zone 1	Rest	Cycle/T-run 90 min/10 min Zone 1-2	10 hr 30 min
		pm			Run 110 min Zone 2		Run 65 min Zone 1-2	Rest		
	Wk 19	am	Swim 60 min Zone 1	Cycle 90 min Zone 2	Swim 60 min Zone 1	Cycle 75 min Zone 1	Swim 60 min Zone 1	Rest	Cycle/T-run 270 min/10 min Zone 1-2	13 hr
		pm	Run 70 min Zone 1		Run 115 min Zone 2		Run 70 min Zone 1-2	Rest		
	Wk 20	am	Swim 50 min Zone 1	Cycle/Run 150 min/60 min Zone 2	Swim 50 min Zone 1	Cycle 60 min Zone 1	Swim 50 min Zone 1	Rest	Cycle/T-run 90 min/10 min Zone 1-2	9 hr 30 min
		pm			Run 60 min Zone 2		Run 60 min Zone 1-2	Rest		
BUILD 3	Wk 21	am	Swim 50 min Zone 1	Cycle 90 min Zone 2	Swim 50 min Zone 1	Cycle 60 min Zone 1	Swim 50 min Zone 1	Rest	Cycle/T-run 285 min/10 min Zone 1-2	12 hr 15 min
		pm	Run 60 min Zone 1		Run 120 min Zone 2		Run 60 min Zone 1-2	Rest		
	Wk 22	am	Swim 50 min Zone 1	Cycle/Run 180 min/70 min Zone 2	Swim 50 min Zone 1	Cycle 60 min Zone 1	Swim 50 min Zone 1	Rest	Cycle/T-run 90 min/5 min Zone 1-2	10 hr
		pm					Run 50 min Zone 1-2	Rest		
PEAK	Wk 23	am	Swim 40 min Zone 1	Cycle 60 min Zone 2	Swim 40 min Zone 1	Cycle 45 min Zone 1	Swim 40 min Zone 1	Rest	Cycle/T-run 60 min/5 min Zone 1-2	6 hr 30
		pm	Run 30 min Zone 1		Run 40 min Zone 2		Run 30 min Zone 1-2	Rest		
RACE	Wk 24	am	Swim 20 min Zone 1	Cycle/Run 40 min/10 min Zone 2	Swim 20 min Zone 1	Cycle 45 min Zone 1	Swim 20 min Zone 1	Cycle/Run 30 min/5 min Zone 1-2	RACE!	3 hr 30 + race
		pm			Run 20 min Zone 2					

First published in 2011 by
New Holland Publishers (UK) Ltd
London • Cape Town • Sydney • Auckland
www.newhollandpublishers.com

Garfield House
86–88 Edgware
Road
London W2 2EA
United Kingdom

80 McKenzie
Street
Cape Town 8001
South Africa

Unit 1, 66
Gibbes Street,
Chatswood
NSW 2067
Australia

218 Lake Road
Northcote
Auckland
New Zealand

A catalogue record for this book is available from the British Library.

ISBN 978 1 84773 995 7

This book has been produced for New Holland Publishers by
Chase My Snail Ltd
London • Cape Town
www.chasemysnail.com

Project Manager and Editor: Daniel Ford
Designer: Darren Exell
Photo Editor: Anthony Ernest
Publisher: Guy Hobbs
Production: Marion Storz
Illustrators: Juliet Percival and James Berrange

2 4 6 8 10 9 7 5 3 1

Reproduction by Pica Digital Pte Ltd, Singapore
Printed and bound in Sngapore by Craft Print International Ltd